RichThoughts
for Breakfast
Volume 5

Harold Herring

President of The Debt Free Army
& RichThoughts TV

www.HaroldHerring.com

Debt Free Army
PO Box 900000, Fort Worth, TX 76161

RichThoughts for Breakfast Volume 5
by Harold Herring

ISBN 978-0-9763668-5-0
Copyright © 2015 by the Debt Free Army
PO Box 900000, Fort Worth, TX 76161
817-222-0011
harold@haroldherring.com

Unless otherwise noted, Scripture references are taken from the King James Version of the Bible.

RichThoughts for Breakfast
Volume 5
Table of Contents

Day	Title	Page
1	7 Things About 911	7
2	Generous, Not Envious	15
3	Suddenly With Abundance	23
4	6 Steps to Success	31
5	Why God Wants You Successful	39
6	7 Keys to Your 100 Fold Harvest	47
7	7 Things Every Sower Should Know	55
8	God Will Flex His Muscles for You	63
9	Success, or Just Getting By	71
10	What Makes a Man Good?	81
11	I Will Make You Rich	91
12	Secrets Revealed and Rewarded	99
13	Visualization and Determination	109
14	8 Things You Ought To Know About You	119
15	7 Questions About the Word and World Economies	127
16	Your Answer Is on the Way	135
17	Why Are You Sleeping With the Frogs?	143
18	Turn Things Around	151
19	A Mind Is a Terrible Thing To Waste	159
20	God Is Going To Pay You	167
21	Who Is God Unwilling To Do Without?	175
22	6 Differences ... Successful and Unsuccessful People	183
23	6 More ... Successful and Unsuccessful People	193
24	God Can Use Anything Anybody Anytime	201
25	7 Surprises God Has For You	209
26	12 Things God Knows About You	217
27	7 Things God Will Do that the Government Can't	225
28	7 Things About God's Will For You	233
29	Write It Down	241
30	Get Out Of Your Rut Now	249
31	When God Takes No Pleasure in You	257

7 Things About 911

I'm convinced that it's time ... really past time for believers who want to avoid a catastrophic financial 9/11 to make a 9-1-1 call to their Heavenly Father.

When you call ... He always answers ... you're one of His favorites.

Jeremiah 33:3 in the Amplified Bible says:

> *"Call to Me and I will answer you and show you great and mighty things, fenced in and hidden, which you do not know (do not distinguish and recognize, have knowledge of and understand)."*

Psalm 50:15 in the New Living Translation says:

> *"Then call on me when you are in trouble, and I will rescue you, and you will give me glory."*

Psalm 34:6-7 in the Message Bible says:

> *"When I was desperate, I called out, and God*

got me out of a tight spot. God's angel sets up a circle of protection around us while we pray."

Psalm 86:7 in the Message Bible says:

"Every time I'm in trouble I call on you, confident that you'll answer."

As I was meditating on the 9-1-1 emergency situations facing many believers, God showed me things we should know.

1. God established a covenant with you to bless you.

The King James Version of the Bible has 280 verses that contain the word *covenant.*

God established a covenant with Noah as he entered the ark (Genesis 6:19) and as he came out.

Genesis 9:11 says:

"And I will establish my covenant with you, neither shall all flesh be cut off any more by the waters of a flood; neither shall there anymore be a flood to destroy the earth."

It seems like a gross understatement to say that when God makes a promise, you can take it to the bank. But that's the reality of Genesis 9:11 which has withstood the test of time.

I do think it's important to remember the first time the word *covenant* is used in the scriptures. That's found in Genesis 9:9 which says:

> *"And I, behold, I establish my covenant with you, and with your seed after you."*

And of course, the second time is in Genesis 9:11.

One of the best protections you can have against adversity (financial or otherwise) or any trick, trap, lie, deception or wile of the enemy is your covenant relationship with the Lord.

If you want to avoid financial snares, make sure you're living a life worthy of your covenant with the Lord.

Truly, the purpose of God's covenant is to bless us so that we can be a blessing to others. Not only does He want to bless us, but He wants us walking in His blessing flow.

1 Peter 3:8 in the Message Bible says:

> *"Summing up:* **Be agreeable, be sympathetic, be loving, be compassionate, be humble.** *That goes for all of you, no exceptions. No retaliation. No sharp-tongued sarcasm. Instead, bless—that's your job, to bless. You'll be a blessing and also get a blessing ..."*

2. You're in the right place at the right time when you obey His Word.

Ecclesiastes 9:11 in the New Living Translation says:

"I have observed something else under the sun. The fastest runner doesn't always win the race, and the strongest warrior doesn't always win the battle. The wise sometimes go hungry, and the skillful are not necessarily wealthy. And those who are educated don't always lead successful lives. It is all decided by chance, by being in the right place at the right time."

God created us as creatures of free will. There are things He has written in our Book of Life, but we determine by our action or inaction whether or not they come to pass.

Romans 9:11 in the Message Bible says:

"What God did in this case made it perfectly plain that his purpose is not a hit-or-miss thing dependent on what we do or don't do, but a sure thing determined by his decision, flowing steadily from his initiative."

Your life is not a game of chance ... **your financial future is not determined by whether or not you win the lottery.** Your future is secured because of your covenant relationship with the Lord and your commitment to do what's right in His sight ... using the wisdom found in His principles.

> 3. **Wisdom from God brings greatness and increase into your life.**

Proverbs 9:11 in the Amplified Bible says:

"For by me [Wisdom from God] your days shall be multiplied, and the years of your life shall be increased."

According to Strong's Concordance the word **multiplied** in the Hebrew means **"to become great."**

When you receive wisdom from God, your days shall become great, and the length of your life shall be increased.

I'd say that's a pretty good combination found in Proverbs 9:11.

4. No medical trauma center can match his 9-1-1 response.

Luke 9:11 says:

"And the people, when they knew it, followed him: and he received them, and spake unto them of the kingdom of God, and healed them that had need of healing."

I think it would be fair to say that even the best hospitals, trauma centers and clinics in the world cannot offer a 100% healing rate.

But Luke 9:11 says that Jesus *"healed them that had need of healing."* The scripture doesn't say He healed most of the people or even the ones with the most serious medical conditions. He healed them ALL regardless of their condition.

We see another 9-1-1 of His healing virtue in John 9:11:

> *"He answered and said, A man that is called Jesus made clay, and anointed mine eyes, and said unto me, Go to the pool of Siloam, and wash: and I went and washed, and I received sight."*

5. The right 9-1-1 call not only sets you free but gives you double for your trouble.

Zechariah 9:11-12 in the Message Bible says:

> *"And you, because of my blood covenant with you, I'll release your prisoners from their hopeless cells. Come home, hope-filled prisoners! This very day I'm declaring a double bonus— everything you lost returned twice-over!"*

No question ... **a 9-1-1 call to God will set you free from what has you bound** ... it will give you hope and, yes, as an extra added benefit ... He will return everything that has been taken from you twice over ... **double for your trouble.**

6. God wants to position you to answer 9-1-1 calls.

One of the clearest reasons God wants to bless you financially is found in 2 Corinthians 9:11 in the Amplified Bible which says:

"Thus you will be enriched in all things and in every way, so that you can be generous, and [your generosity as it is] administered by us will bring forth thanksgiving to God."

God wants to enrich you ... not just so you can have a Lear Jet and a Corvette ... though He's not against that. **He wants to bless you so that you can be generous to others who may be going through their own 9-1-1 emergency.**

The last sentence in the New Living Translation of 2 Corinthians 9:11 says:

"... Yes, you will be enriched in every way so that you can always be generous. And when we take your gifts to those who need them, they will thank God."

As you bless others ... they will Praise God for getting them out of a tight spot.

7. Tell the world about God's 9-1-1 response to the adversities in your life.

Psalm 9:11 in the New Living Translation says:

"Sing praises to the Lord who reigns in Jerusalem. Tell the world about his unforgettable

deeds."

If you've ever made a call to 9-1-1 ... the immediate response of emergency personnel was no doubt a blessing to you. It's something that you will talk about for years to come.

As God has responded to every 9-1-1 call you've ever made ... you should be singing His praises and rejoicing that He is always there for you ... so that others will know how good your God is.

Day 2

Generous, Not Envious

Are you *"envious because I am generous"*?

As I read those words in Matthew 20:13-15 in the New International Version, my spirit was stirred. Here's what the complete passage says:

> *"But he answered one of them, 'Friend, I am not being unfair to you. Didn't you agree to work for a denarius? Take your pay and go. I want to give the man who was hired last the same as I gave you. Don't I have the right to do what I want with my own money? Or are you envious because I am generous?' "*

Don't be envious ... be generous. Don't be that ... be this.

In this scripture Jesus is concluding the parable about the vineyard owner who hired workers in the early morning for the wage of a denarius (one penny) for a day's labor. The scripture says they were agreed on this wage.

Matthew 20:1-2 tells us:

"For the kingdom of heaven is like unto a man that is a householder, which went out early in the morning to hire labourers into his vineyard. And when he had agreed with the labourers for a penny a day, he sent them into his vineyard."

Three hours later, the landowner went to the market-place, saw some other "idle" workers standing around ... he hired them and said, "Whatsoever is right I will give you." (Matthew 20:4)

Matthew 20:5 in the Contemporary English Version says:

"At noon (sixth hour) and again about three in the afternoon (ninth hour) he returned to the market. And each time he made the same agreement with others who were loafing around with nothing to do."

In Matthew 20:6 we read where the vineyard owner at 5 PM (eleventh hour) went back to the marketplace where he found four men still standing around, and he asked the men why they hadn't been working that day.

The response is found in Matthew 20:7. The Amplified Bible says:

"They answered him, Because nobody has hired us. He told them, You go out into the vineyard

also and you will get whatever is just and fair."

One hour later, at 6 PM when the work day was completed, the vineyard owner told the foreman to pay the men ... beginning with the one-hour workers. These men were paid a full day's wage of one denarius.

There are several things at work in the passage of scripture dealing with the men who only worked one hour.

First, they had been at the marketplace early in the morning (6 AM) looking for work.

Second, these men had been passed over for work at 9 AM, noon and 3 PM.

Third, even though the work day was one hour from being over, there were four men still standing in the marketplace hoping to find some work ... some pay was better than none at all, for the scripture says in Verse 6 that they had been there all day.

Fourth, these men didn't give up hope ... **they stayed around**. If these four workers hadn't been picked on the four previous times ... it's fair to assume that perhaps they weren't the prime choice for workers.

This point is not clearly made in scripture, but I do think it's a reasonable assumption since they were there to be chosen ... perhaps they were older or had some physical aliment that made them less attractive as day laborers. Regardless, they were willing to work because they needed a penny that day.

Fifth and finally, the owner of the vineyard put people ahead of profits ... he had a generous heart.

Next, the foreman paid the three-hour workers a denarius, so I'm sure word spread down the line, and the nine- and twelve-hour workers began to assume they would be paid more ... because they had worked longer.

Matthew 20:8-12 in the New Living Translation says:

"That evening he told the foreman to call the workers in and pay them, beginning with the last workers first. When those hired at five o'clock were paid, each received a full day's wage. When those hired first came to get their pay, they assumed they would receive more. But they, too, were paid a day's wage. <u>*When they received their pay, they protested to the owner, 'Those people worked only one hour, and yet you've paid them just as much as you paid us who worked all day in the scorching heat.'*</u> *"*

Now let's look at Matthew 20:13-15 in the New International Version one more time.

"But he answered one of them, 'Friend, I am not being unfair to you. Didn't you agree to work for a

denarius? Take your pay and go. I want to give the man who was hired last the same as I gave you. Don't I have the right to do what I want with my own money? Or are you envious because I am generous?' "

Sadly, there are workers ... people ... yes, even Christians who don't mind other people being blessed as long as the others aren't blessed more than they are.

There are workers ... people ... yes, even Christians who don't mind other people succeeding as long as the others aren't more successful than they are.

It's not good to assume too much, but the scripture indicates the last four workers were not picked but were there all day. Therefore, it's safe to wonder if they were perhaps the least desirable workers ... maybe it was their age or physical condition ... but the twelve-hour workers showed no mercy or concern for them. They were thinking of themselves.

Truthfully, **the right kind of attitude would have been one of thankfulness that these four workers had been blessed to provide for their families**. But that is not the natural reaction, which in this case is described as jealousy.

It just occurred to me that the problem with these workers may go even deeper than jealousy. **The men questioned the householder's plans to spend his** money the way he saw fit, which was really questioning his authority.

Submission to authority is a powerful spiritual concept which I don't have time to share in this teaching.

For the purpose of discussion in this teaching let me simply say that **those who don't understand how to operate under authority will never be given authority over others.**

Submission to authority is never jealous. It's also important to understand that someone who claims to be submitted to authority is never proven when things are going the way they think they should. They merely agree to submit because they find nothing wrong.

The real test of a person's submission to authority is their reaction when things are not going the way they want or think they should.

More on authority ... on another day.

Back to the parable ... when a worker ... even a Christian ... is found looking at what other people have ... then that person will not be satisfied with what they have. **Jealousy is a trap that causes much trouble.**

I can tell you that the proper response to others' good fortune is to rejoice over what they've been given.

Romans 12:15 in the Amplified Bible says:

"Rejoice with those who rejoice [sharing others' joy], and weep with those who weep [sharing others' grief]."

Here's a spiritual truth that each of us should get deep down inside of us.

When we can get as excited about other people's blessings as we are our own, WATCH OUT, because our blessings and victories are right behind us ... about to overtake us.

Being excited for others' blessings is a spiritual dynamic that must be satisfied before any of us will walk in abundant blessings.

If you want to be chosen ... never compare and compete with others ... be happy for those who are blessed.

Our attitude and obedience to authority will determine our blessings.

Always be generous ... and never envious. In other words ... be this (generous) not that (envious).

Day
3

Suddenly With Abundance

Let me just tell you … by the time we finish our reading today you'll be shouting Hallelujah.

2 Chronicles 29:36 tells us:

> *"And Hezekiah rejoiced, and all the people, that God had prepared the people: for the thing was done suddenly."*

The word "suddenly" is in the King James Version of the Bible a total of 40 times, the Amplified Bible, a total of 60 times, and the New Living Translation a total of 101 times.

But "suddenly" I felt directed to read 2 Chronicles 29:34, 35 and then 36 again.

> "But the priests were too few, so that they could not flay all the burnt offerings: wherefore their brethren the Levites did help them, till the work was ended, and until the other priests had

sanctified themselves: for the Levites were more upright in heart to sanctify themselves than the priests.

"And also the burnt offerings were in abundance, with the fat of the peace offerings, and the drink offerings for every burnt offering. So the service of the house of the LORD was set in order.

"And Hezekiah rejoiced, and all the people, that God had prepared the people: for the thing was done suddenly."

While "suddenly" is the focus of this teaching ... several other important thoughts began stirring in my spirit ... as I read this passage.

Did you notice in Verse 34 the scripture says "the priests were too few"? To me the message is very clear.

The first thing God wants ... is for you and me to be involved in His work. That's His plan. **If you have a pulse, you have a purpose.**

If you have a pulse ... you have a purpose.

WRITE IT DOWN ... PLEASE ... GET IT DOWN IN YOUR SPIRIT ... PLEASE ...

The preparation and presentation of the gospel to a lost and dying world is not just the function of pastors

… it's an on-the-job description of EVERY born-again believer. (2 Corinthians 3:6; Revelation 1:6; 5:10)

Sometimes we're willing to give a brother or sister a word of encouragement in the midst of their adversity … if that's all it is, a word. But should they need more encouragement … more of our time … then we're all too often a bit hesitant.

Bottom line … there are times when we're happy, in fact, eager to give folks our opinions but reluctant to give them our time.

Make no mistake about it … God wants us involved in the work of the ministry. It doesn't matter whether we have Reverend, Elder, Pastor, Apostle or Bishop stuck in front of our name.

1 Corinthians 12:25 in the Amplified Bible says:

> *"So that there should be no division or discord or lack of adaptation [of the parts of the body to each other], but the members all alike should have a mutual interest in and care for one another."*

We're to have a "mutual interest in and care for one another." That seems plain to me.

When WE give a word of encouragement, pray with or give counsel to someone else … we are lifting them up.

But in reality, if we're lifting them up ... encouraging them, praying for them, counseling them, blessing them ... then we are also lifting up ourselves.

That should be a totally separate teaching ... which I'll do in the next few days.

The second thing He wants you to realize is when you get involved with God's plan, abundance will be realized in God's House and in His children.

In 2 Chronicles 29:35 it says there was an abundance of offerings.

When you reach out to help others ... when you do what may not be convenient at the moment, even if it was God-directed ... then you will find an abundance to sow as an offering.

2 Corinthians 9:8 in the New Living Translation says:

> *"And God will generously provide all you need. Then you will always have everything you need and plenty left over to share with others."*

We will not only find abundance ... but, the blessings of the Lord will begin to overtake us.

Deuteronomy 28:2 says:

> *"And all these blessings shall come upon you and overtake you if you heed the voice of the*

Lord your God."

Have you ever been walking along … tithing and giving offerings … doing what the Word has directed you to do … yet wondering where the blessings of the Lord are?

When you feel all alone … when you feel like nothing is working … you've got to know that the sound you hear is the blessing of the Lord coming up behind you ready to overtake you … and it's going to happen SUDDENLY.

The third thing God wants you to know is that your victory will come suddenly.

As a reminder 2 Chronicles 29:36 says:

"And Hezekiah rejoiced, and all the people, that God had prepared the people: for the thing was done suddenly."

How does God prepare you? Through obedience.

If you're doing what He's asked you to do … when He asks you to do it and where He wants you to do it … then you will experience "sudden" manifestation and victory over every attack of the enemy.

Psalm 6:10 in the New Living Translation says:

"May all my enemies be disgraced and terrified. May they suddenly turn back in shame."

In Joshua 11:6 it says:

"And the LORD said unto Joshua, Be not afraid because of them: for to morrow about this time will I deliver them up all slain before Israel: thou shalt hough their horses, and burn their chariots with fire."

Hallelujah ... by this time tomorrow ... all your enemies will be DEAD.

Joshua got a SUDDEN VICTORY over His enemies, and God wants to do the same thing for you.

"Yes, but Brother Harold, I don't have any enemies."

Oh? Yes, you do.

- Debt is an enemy.
- Lack is an enemy.
- Sickness is an enemy.
- Depression is an enemy.
- Strife is an enemy.

God will give you a sudden victory over every attack of the enemy, but you must be obedient and pliable in His hands.

Your obedience will always bring you the victories you need and desire ... plus they will come suddenly just as God has promised.

Isaiah 48:3 in the New Living Translation says:

> *"Long ago I told you what was going to happen. Then **suddenly** I took action, and all my predictions came true."*

If you need SUDDEN Manifestation in your life … then rely on the Holy Spirit for direction.

Acts 2:1-4 says:

> *"And when the day of Pentecost was fully come, they were all with one accord in one place.*
>
> *"**And suddenly there came a sound from heaven as of a rushing mighty wind, and it filled all the house where they were sitting**.*
>
> *"And there appeared unto them cloven tongues like as of fire, and it sat upon each of them.*
>
> *"And they were all filled with the Holy Ghost, and began to speak with other tongues, as the Spirit gave them utterance."*

The Holy Spirit came suddenly … He will comfort and direct you in all wisdom and victory.

Child of God, the thing that stirred in me today … is that God wants to SUDDENLY move on your behalf … but your life has to line up with the Word.

You will have to help where He says help … do what

He says to do and give where, when and whatever He tells you to give.

The scripture is filled with SUDDEN victories and breakthroughs over attacks of the enemy.

Luke 24:31 in the New Living Translation says:

"Suddenly, their eyes were opened, and they recognized him ..."

As a minister of God's Word, I want you to recognize the seasons, moves and blessings of God. My prayer for you is to see your surroundings with the eye of the spirit and not that of your natural mind.

Day 4

6 Steps to Success

If you'll think seriously with me for a moment, you will realize that you are one of two kinds of people.

You are either a "can do" person or you are a "can't do" person.

If you feel you can't do things, <u>I'm going to give you six points that will take you out of the loser's circle and put you into the winner's circle</u>.

No matter how unsuccessful you may have been up to this point, it can change today.

All of the success strategies known to the world have their basis ... their foundation ... in the Bible.

These six things will make you a winner in your career, in your marriage, in any project you do, or in any other aspect of your life.

The major accomplishments in life usually pivot around several fairly simple rules.

We need to realize that everything that amazes us

today … was only a thought … an idea to someone else at another time.

When we read about jets that go six hundred MPH and travel five miles above the earth, we have to remember that it all began with the idea that it "could" work.

The first thing we have to do if we're going to be successful at any given thing is to fix our minds on what we want to do ... our objective.

The Bible tells us that a double-minded man is unstable in all of his ways.

James 1:8 in the Amplified Bible says:

> *"[For being as he is] a man of two minds (hesitating, dubious, irresolute), [he is] unstable and unreliable and uncertain about everything [he thinks, feels, decides]."*

You can do something every day, but you can't do everything every day.

You are going to have to decide what you specifically want to do.

Many times you hear people say they are going to be whatever God wants them to be. That sounds very spiritual, but it doesn't work.

In Ecclesiastes 9:10, the first part of that scripture says:

> *"Whatsoever thy hand findeth to do, do it with thy might."*

The Bible is telling you that whatever you plan to do, get in there and do it. Be specific about it, and do it.

The remainder of Ecclesiastes 9:10 brings out a very good point:

> *"… for there is no work, nor device, nor knowledge, nor wisdom, in the grave, wither thou goest."*

The point of this scripture is you can only accomplish things on the earth while you are living, so you'd better get to it.

The second thing it takes to be a success is determining what it will cost to accomplish the desired goal.

You are going to have to pay a price.

Do you see all the gimmicks around offering things for free? You are going to have to realize that nothing is free.

The scriptures prepare us to make a commitment. Look at Luke 14:28-30 in the New Living Translation:

"But don't begin until you count the cost. For who would begin construction of a building without first calculating the cost to see if there is enough money to finish it? Otherwise, you might complete only the foundation before running out of money, and then everyone would laugh at you. They would say, 'There's the person who started that building and couldn't afford to finish it!' "

You have to be willing to pay the price for your success. Just ask any athlete how much time they spend in preparation for each minute on the court or playing field.

Third, establish a timetable in which to accomplish specific goals. This is a hard thing for some people to get established.

The goals set for this ministry took time and effort. It wasn't accomplished out on the golf course even though I lived on the tenth hole of a course. I only played golf on that course four times in nine years ... because I had other priorities that kept taking precedent.

The fourth step is developing a workable game plan.

You can't always write a workable game plan the

first time you sit down. You may not know all the steps it takes, but you write it out the best you can figure. Then, adjust it and readjust it as necessary.

After a few years you will be a pro at writing out a game plan for being successful at what you have chosen to do, whatever that might be. **You will see it accomplished, but you have to be flexible in your game plan.**

This is where it's important to have friends/mentors that share your motivation. **You can brainstorm with them about possibilities.**

Proverbs 27:17 in the Amplified Bible says:

"Iron sharpens iron; so a man sharpens the countenance of his friend [to show rage or worthy purpose]."

Fifth, put your plan or goal into a tangible form.

You have to write the vision and make it plain. This step is critically important.

For years I used legal pads for preparing my Critical Path, which is what I call my tangible form.

Now I'm using "Mind Map" which is an excellent computer program for brainstorming and planning.

Number six is the one that will make all the difference in the world if you are a child of God.

Decide how you plan to use your success for God and see the tangible form each day. This is the thing that is missing in the world's system of success.

People may achieve their success, but too many of them end up divorced or in drug or alcohol addiction. They end up unhappy because Satan has plans to make them captive to their success.

As a child of God you can enjoy great success if you will decide now what your success is going to do for God. If you do that, you can have all the success that you have the nerve to ask God for. But you are going to have to do all six things.

You have to be single of mind.

Luke 9:62 in the New Living Translation says:

"But Jesus told him, 'Anyone who puts a hand to the plow and then looks back is not fit for the Kingdom of God.' "

God is not interested in double-minded people. He is interested in people that pick up the plow and finish the job.

Let me show you a promise that you will be glad you looked at. Matthew 17:20 says:

"And Jesus said unto them, ... If ye have faith as a grain of mustard seed, ye shall say unto this mountain, Remove hence to yonder place; and it

shall remove; and nothing shall be impossible unto you."

Pay particular attention to that last part.

"… and nothing shall be impossible unto you."

Did you catch this? Nothing will be impossible to you.

You have to believe that you are going to succeed.

Remember what Ecclesiastes 9:10 says:

"Whatsoever thy hand findeth to do, do it with thy might …"

Let's look at the 6 steps to success one more time.

1. Fix in your mind on exactly what you want to accomplish.

2. Determine what it will cost to accomplish the desired goal.

3. Establish a timetable with definite goals that you want to reach.

4. Set up a workable game plan, but be sure it is flexible.

5. Turn your plan or desired goal into a tangible form.

6. Decide how you plan to use the success that you accomplish for God and look at it each day.

Remember, Jesus asked a man to follow him, and the man said, "Let me go home and bury my father first."

Jesus replied to him, "Let the dead bury the dead." (Taken from Matthew 8:22; Luke 9:60)

Jesus said the man was not worthy. **You have to be willing to give up everything**. You have to say, "I'm going on no matter what." That's the point you have to come to in your life.

Once you are awakened and enlightened to the fact that your life is nothing without Jesus, success can and will be yours.

Day 5

Why God Wants You Successful

There is absolutely no doubt that God wants you manifesting biblical success in your life.

It's important to understand the significance of biblical success ... that's where you and everyone around you ... recognizes that God makes you successful.

Deuteronomy 30:9 in the New Century Version says:

> *"The Lord your God will make you successful in everything you do. You will have many children, your cattle will have many calves, and your fields will produce good crops, because the Lord will again be happy with you, just as he was with your ancestors."*

Did you notice that the first sentence in this passage of scripture says: *"The Lord your God will make you successful in everything you do ..."*

First off, He's not just any God. He's your God ... your personal God ... the one who has your

picture on His refrigerator.

Second, He will make you successful in EVERY-THING you do. Not just some things. Or the most pressing or important things. No, He, the Lord God Almighty, is going to make you successful in ALL you do.

> The key to our biblical success is our obedience to His instructions.

Joshua 1:7 in the New Century Version says:

> *"Be strong and brave. Be sure to obey all the teachings my servant Moses gave you. If you follow them exactly, you will be successful in everything you do."*

Our obedience to God's instructions as a prerequisite for our success is mentioned several other times in scripture as well.

1 Kings 2:3 in the New Century Version says:

> *"Obey the Lord your God. Follow him by obeying his demands, his commands, his laws, and his rules that are written in the teachings of Moses. If you do these things, you will be successful in all you do and wherever you go."*

When we're obedient to His Word ... then we will

experience biblical success regardless of where we're at or what we're going through.

Job 8:7 in the New Century Version says:

> *"Where you began will seem unimportant, because your future will be so successful."*

Joseph was prosperous ... a successful man even when he was standing on a slave block in Egypt.

Genesis 39:2 in the New Century Version says:

> *"The Lord was with Joseph, and he became a successful man. He lived in the house of his master, Potiphar the Egyptian."*

The King James Version of Genesis 39:2 says that Joseph was a prosperous man.

At this very moment ... you can be up to your eyeballs in debt ... working a dead-end job ... so broke you can't rub two pennies together ... but that's not where you're going to stay ... when you follow God's principles of biblical success.

Genesis 39:3 in the New Century Version says:

> *"Potiphar saw that the Lord was with Joseph and that the Lord made Joseph successful in everything he did."*

> **Everywhere Joseph went people were blessed**. He was successful regardless of his circumstances.

Genesis 39:23 in the New Century Version says:

"The warden paid no attention to anything that was in Joseph's care because the Lord was with Joseph and made him successful in everything he did."

It's not where you're at … it's where you're going.

I want you to write this next statement down …

It's not where I'm at … it's where I'm going.

You can even personalize it.

It's not where [Name] is at … it's where [Name] is going.

Let's look at **sixteen key principles to guide you on your journey to biblical success.**

1. Biblical success is a multiplier … it's contagious and impacts everyone who comes near it.

2. Biblical success unites, it doesn't divide.

3. Biblical success is a long-range solution to

every problem you face.

4. Biblical success is God's plan to bless you, which enables you to bless others.

5. Biblical success creates opportunities for personal growth, advancement and scriptural giving.

6. **Biblical success is not about you but what He can do through you.**

7. Biblical success demotes greed and promotes generosity.

8. Biblical success is a consequence of the decisions you make and the actions you take.

9. Biblical success experienced by the few is designed to bless the many who have not yet come into a revelation of His biblical rewards.

10. When governments seek to excessively tax or control the earnings of those who experience biblical success ... the ultimate victims will not be the rich but the poor who are the recipients of their charity.

11. Biblical success is based on your understanding and activation of the timeless principles found in His Word.

12. Biblical success isn't the pursuit of wealth but

rather the accomplishment of Godly goals.

13. Biblical success isn't against you being rich but rather you being controlled by riches.

14. Biblical success is knowing that ... what you've got is not all you'll ever have ... and what you're doing at the moment is NOT all you'll ever do.

15. Biblical success is not what you have but rather who has you.

16. **Biblical success is optional, but so is failure.**

In order to experience biblical success ... there are some things you must start doing ... obeying God's instructions ... and some things you must stop doing ... things that you must let exit out of your life.

Success in Spanish is the word "éxito."

If you want to be a success in life you have to exit and escape from some of your previous habits and acquaintances.

You must leave the poverty mentality to enter into His plan for your biblical success.

You must leave thoughts of limitation behind ... to enter the reality of biblical success.

You must leave the blame game ... and enter into a

new era of personal accountability for your actions.

You must leave behind any tolerance of mediocrity … to enter a lifestyle of excellence.

You must begin to see success as a way out of everything that has been holding you back and keeping you down.

When you start doing what's right in God's eyes, then biblical success is your ultimate destination.

So one final question:

Why does God want you … one person … to be successful?

The same reason God wanted King David successful and prosperous … so His people can be blessed.

2 Samuel 5:12 in the Good News Translation says:

> *"And so David realized that the Lord had established him as king of Israel and was making his kingdom prosperous for the sake of his people."*

When you're successful … other people are blessed by their association with you. Even the heathen will rejoice in God.

Genesis 39:5 says:

> *"And it came to pass from the time that he had made him overseer in his house, and over all that he had, that the LORD blessed the Egyptian's house for Joseph's sake; and the blessing of the LORD was upon all that he had in the house, and in the field."*

God wants you successful for a reason ... but it's your decision whether or not His desire for you becomes a reality.

Day 6

7 Keys to Your 100 Fold Harvest

Matthew 13:23 says:

> *"But he that received seed into the good ground is he that heareth the word, and understandeth it; which also beareth fruit, and bringeth forth, some an hundredfold, some sixty, some thirty."*

Here are seven keys to your hundredfold harvest.

1. Where does the seed you sow come from?

In the parable of the sower there are three verses (Matthew 13:19, 22-23) where we're told that the sower received seed.

The question I'm prompted to ask is where did the sower receive seed from?

2 Corinthians 9:10 in the Amplified Bible says:

> *"And [God] Who provides seed for the sower and bread for eating will also provide and multiply your [resources for] sowing and increase the*

fruits of your righteousness [which manifests it-self in active goodness, kindness, and charity]."

God provides seed to the sower.

The criteria for receiving seed to sow is that you are a sower. The immediate response of some would be ... "Yes, but I have nothing to sow."

You have something to sow ... but at the moment you may be sowing it to the credit card company ... the mortgage company ... the automobile finance company ... the big screen TV company ... the time share company ... the boat company, and the list goes on.

People have something to sow ... but at some point, **they made a conscious decision to sow their seed into things with interest charges ... where their seed will never EVER produce a harvest.**

God is going to give seed to the sower. Not only is He going to give seed to the sower, but He is going to multiply it.

2 Corinthians 9:10 in the Amplified Bible says:

*"And [God] Who provides seed for the sower and bread for eating will also provide and **multiply your [resources for] sowing** and increase the fruits of your righteousness [which manifests itself in active goodness, kindness, and charity]."*

2. You must sow in good ground.

According to Strong's Concordance the word *good* in Matthew 13:23 is the Greek word **kalos** (G2570) which means:

"beautiful, excellent, eminent, choice, surpassing, precious, useful, suitable, commendable, admirable; excellent in its nature and characteristics ..."

I think it's fair to say that "good ground" is where you can find a church, ministry or organization where the leadership is excellent in its operation … honoring the precious seeds with which it's entrusted … and who will mentally and spiritually come into agreement with you confirming their faith with yours.

It's spiritually unwise to ask someone who doesn't believe in biblical prosperity to come into agreement with you for a hundredfold return on a seed you've sown with them. They will gladly receive your seed but without the power of agreement.

3. If you aren't listening for the truth you'll never hear it.

Matthew 13:23 says:

"But he that received seed into the good ground is he that heareth the word …"

There are two things that stirred in me as I read this passage …

First, you have to put yourself in a position to hear the truth.

If you're attending a high-steeple, few-people church where the fullness of the gospel is never taught, or if you never read books written by men and women of God with a revelatory understanding of the Word ... who teach the word on TV or over the Internet ... then you're not in a position to receive the truth.

Second, you need to keep hearing and hearing the precious promises of God.

Romans 10:17 says:

"So then faith cometh by hearing, and hearing by the word of God."

4. If you don't understand the hundredfold ... you'll never manifest it.

Matthew 13:23 says:

"But he that received seed into the good ground is he that <u>heareth</u> the word, and <u>understandeth</u> it ..."

It's not just enough to hear the Word ... you must understand it as well.

Jesus understood this distinction. Matthew 15:10 says:

*"And he called the multitude, and said unto them, Hear, **and understand."***

Hearing is an audible reception of words spoken … understanding is the mental recognition of what you've just heard and what needs to be done … and doing it.

Jesus made a definite distinction between hearing and understanding. The scripture is also very clear about the consequences of hearing but not understanding what the Word has to say.

Matthew 13:19 in the New Living Translation says:

"The seed that fell on the footpath represents those who hear the message about the Kingdom and don't understand it. Then the evil one comes and snatches away the seed that was planted in their hearts."

5. If you're not productive there's no reason for you to be around.

Matthew 13:23 says:

"But he that received seed into the good ground is he that heareth the word, and understandeth it; which also beareth fruit …"

Bearing fruit is not optional … in fact, it is an absolute requirement.

John 15:2 in the Amplified Bible says:

> *"Any branch in Me that does not bear fruit [that stops bearing] He cuts away (trims off, takes away); and He cleanses and repeatedly prunes every branch that continues to bear fruit, to make it bear more and richer and more excellent fruit."*

Being not just a sower but one who produces fruit is not just something that's nice and desirable … it is a necessity for our survival and favor in God's eyes.

We're either producing harvests, or we're cut off. Truly, God wants around Him people who understand seed-time and harvest … people who know the value of sowing seeds … people who have expectation for harvests.

6. Better than Wall Street and/or the lottery … some 30, 60, 100 fold.

Matthew 13:23 says:

> *"But he that received seed into the good ground is he that heareth the word, and understandeth it; which also beareth fruit, and bringeth forth, some an <u>hundredfold</u>, some <u>sixty</u>, some <u>thirty</u>."*

Sometimes your return is thirtyfold, sometimes it is

sixtyfold. However, **if you walk faithfully in God's principles of seedtime and harvest, your return will always be hundredfold** – the best possible return under the circumstances.

One hundred is a unique number. It is the only number that can represent many other numbers. Not only does it mean one hundred, it can also signify that something is complete, whole, or the best possible.

7. What you sow is what you're going to reap.

Matthew 13:23 in the New Living Translation says:

"The seed that fell on good soil represents those who truly hear and understand God's word and produce a harvest of thirty, sixty, or even a hundred times as much as had been planted!"

The key phrase in this verse is that the sower received "… as much as had been planted."

The size of the harvest you receive is determined by the amount that you sow. Not what you need … but what you sow.

Galatians 6:7 in the Amplified Bible says:

"Do not be deceived and deluded and misled; God will not allow Himself to be sneered at (scorned, disdained, or mocked by mere pretensions or professions, or by His precepts being set aside.) [He inevitably deludes himself who

attempts to delude God.] For whatever a man sows, that and that only is what he will reap."

Pay particular attention to the last sentence in this verse.

"… For whatever a man sows, that and that only is what he will reap."

You will reap what you've sown.

For instance, **nothing times 30, 60 or 100 still equals nothing.**

If you plant nothing … your multiplied harvest will still be nothing.

However, if you plant $100 … then God's multiplication table will bring forth a harvest of $3,000; $6,000; $10,000 or the perfect yield for the seed sown … the best possible harvest.

Is this the day … for you to plant a 30, 60, 100 fold seed into the ministry of the Debt Free Army … if you feel so led, go to www.haroldherring.com and sow according to your expectation for a harvest.

Day 7

7 Things Every Sower Should Know

I grew up in eastern North Carolina at a time when it was primarily an agricultural economy. So, I have a little more than a basic understanding of seedtime and harvest.

There are seven key things every sower should know if they want to receive a proper harvest.

#1—The Soil Must Be Prepared for the Seed

My parents worked as sharecroppers until I was about four years of age. Our home was off the highway up in the fields. We didn't have electricity or indoor plumbing.

I remember playing at the end of the rows while my **Daddy and Momma would turn the soil for whichever crop they were about to plant.**

When my fine wife, Bev, and I moved into a home in Fort Worth a number of years ago, one of the first things she did was have the soil prepared so she could plant her flower seeds around the house.

Soil must be prepared to receive the seed, and Jesus compares the soil to our hearts' condition. Just as the earth is prepared, so we must prepare our hearts before the first seed is ever sown.

#2—The Right Seed at the Right Time

Some years ago, I saw a most interesting and entertaining movie called *Secondhand Lions*. In fact, I bought the movie and have watched it numerous times.

In the movie there are **two elderly brothers who are sold a bunch of seed.** They thought the seeds would produce a variety of vegetables in their garden. However, in a rather humorous scene, they discovered that all the seeds were the same.

You cannot sow watermelon seeds and expect to harvest ears of corn. **You must have the right kind of seed for a proper harvest.**

Genesis 1:11-12 says:

> *"And God said, Let the earth bring forth grass, the herb yielding seed, and the fruit tree after his kind … and the tree yielding fruit, whose seed was in itself, after his kind: and God saw that it was good."*

God thinks it's good when everything reproduces after its own kind.

If you sow apple seeds you will reap apples. Sow oranges, and you will reap oranges.

Everything reproduces after its own kind. That's a natural law that every person accepts regardless of spiritual knowledge.

John 3:6 says:

> *"That which is born of the flesh is flesh; and that which is born of the Spirit is spirit."*

But you and I, **as believers, have a better covenant.** We also have the spirit of God.

John 15:7 says:

> *"If ye abide in me and my words abide in ye, ask what you will and it shall be given unto you."*

That's why it's so important that we sow the right seed at the right time in the right place. It wouldn't do you any good to sow the right seed at the wrong time.

For instance, there is no need to sow some seeds during the winter months in areas where the ground cannot receive it because it's cold and/or frozen.

We should always allow the Spirit of God to direct where we plant our seeds.

When we move in direct obedience to His divine direction, then we will always experience supernatural increase.

#3—The Right Ingredients

In order to produce a bumper crop harvest, it's imperative that you have the proper nutrients to spur growth while destroying weeds and harmful predators like bugs and animals that might ruin your crop.

In your giving, you're faced with another harmful predator, one that seeks to undermine every decision you make. This enemy, the devil, will use every trick, trap, lie and deception, hoping you'll fall for them.

If you want to produce a bumper crop harvest ... you must have a good supply of nutrients.

With regards to the seeds you sow, having the proper nutrients will determine the success of your harvest.

Your soil must be rich enough to grow your crop of choice, otherwise you must add the nutrients it needs.

It's also imperative that you properly use the mental nutrients of attitude and confession which will dramatically impact the harvest of your life.

That's why you must renew your mind with His precious promises. **If you don't use the right nutrients, then you will experience crop failure.** However, a

right mixture of spiritual nutrients will bring you a harvest far greater than Miracle Grow.

Write out the scriptures that encourage you in your wait between seedtime and harvest.

<u>Feeding your spirit with these nutrients from the Word will ensure your success and strengthen your faith</u>.

You can't have faith for what you don't have knowledge of ...

#4—The Proper Use of Water

<u>I learned as a boy that you can drown a crop by giving it too much water</u>. **It's also important that you use pure water. Salt water, for instance, would kill any crop.**

Ephesians 5:26 says:

> *"That he might sanctify and cleanse it with the washing of water by the word."*

The proper application of water ... at the right time and in the right amount as directed by the Spirit will ensure the harvest.

Isaiah 44:3 says:

> *"For I will pour water upon him that is thirsty, and floods upon the dry ground: I will pour my spirit upon thy seed, and my blessing upon thine*

offspring."

#5—The Right Kind of Light.

You would probably assume that I'm just talking about sunshine, but that's not necessarily so. In certain parts of the country they get very little sustained sunshine during certain times of the year ... because of the rain.

Some of the most beautiful flowers are grown in hot houses where there is little sunshine. The bottom line is this ... regardless of the source ... light produces energy in a plant.

Light also produces a spiritual energy ... that empowers you for great success.

Proverbs 4:18 says:

> *"But the path of the just is as the shining light, that shineth more and more unto the perfect day."*

In tending the seed that you've sown for a harvest ... **you need the light of His Word to direct you in every area of your life.**

Psalm 119:105 says:

> *"Thy word is a lamp unto my feet, and a light unto my path."*

Without the light ... plants will die ... without His

life … all of us will perish.

#6—Loving Care

It's important for every farmer … every person who sows … to provide loving care and oversight of what they've planted.

For instance, if you plant a vegetable garden, you must make sure the plants are properly watered. You must make sure all the weeds are removed. This is not a one-time event. Weeds are sneaky … they'll show up when you least expect them.

When it comes to the weeds attacking the seeds that you've sown … sometimes they manifest in the form of family members or friends. These weeds speak doubt and despair. If you love your seed … you can't allow weeds to flourish. Your loving protection is essential to the growth of your seed.

#7—Good Air

Here's a scientific fact … **the seventh critical ingredient to produce a crop is air. CO_2 or carbon dioxide can poison and kill you, but it is just what plants need to flourish.** In return, they release oxygen which is just what we need to breathe. The right kind of air is important to everyone. In other words, having the right stuff present allows us all to reap an abundant harvest of blessings.

In His wisdom, God has provided it all … in the earth

and in the spirit. It's up to us to put those principles into action for an abundant life.

And I could add #8 … if you don't sow … you won't reap.

Day 8

God Will Flex His Muscles for You

Have you ever been really thirsty on a hot summer's day?

I'm talking about your throat being as dry as a West Texas tumbleweed being swept through the wide-open prairie.

Finally, after what seems like the longest time, you wrap your hands around a glass of cool water. After that first long sip ... you take the glass from your mouth and you say, "Ah."

Simply said, at last you have found relief from your dry and desperate condition.

Ah means **satisfaction in knowing that what was a trying circumstance has been turned completely around** ... that you now have relief from what felt like a seemingly impossible problem.

Have you been dealing with a serious lack in your finances or a drastic drop in your investment portfolio or retirement income?

Have you been dealing with the longest period of unemployment in your life or perhaps an attack on your health or someone who's close to you?

Does it seem that you've been spiritually dry, and that you've gone too long without feeling His presence or power?

If you've answered yes to any of these questions ... then you can relax in Him; as Jeremiah 32:17 is bringing you the confidence, the knowledge and the promised relief from your financial, physical, mental and spiritual drought.

> *"Ah Lord GOD! behold, thou hast made the heaven and the earth by thy great power and stretched out arm, and there **is nothing** too hard for thee."*

You can find relief in a lot of places ... humanitarian programs, governmental agencies ... even friends or family ... but there is one source of relief that is beyond any other, and it's permanent.

> *"Ah Lord GOD!"*

That's the kind of relief I'm talking about.

This verse goes on to talk about God's power of creation ... how He spoke the earth and everything in it ... into existence.

God's power is His words, for His Words contain life.

John 6:63 says:

> *"… the words that I speak unto you, they are spirit and they are life."*

Yet, the verse in Jeremiah 32:17 says that He made:

> *"… the heaven and the earth by [His] great power and stretched out arm …"*

God spoke the world into existence … so the question I have is … why would it be necessary for God to bring relief by His *stretched out arm*?

In Strong's Concordance the Hebrew word for *stretched out* is **natah** (H5186). This particular Hebrew word appears in the King James Version of the Bible a total of 216 times in 207 verses, and it means:

"to stretch out, extend, spread out, pitch, turn, incline, bend down, hold out, extend or influence."

As I read and re-read this verse … it occurred to me that **God, the creator of heaven and earth, is using His creative power working on your behalf.**

Figuratively speaking, it's like God, Elohim, the Almighty One is rolling up His heavenly sleeves and is going to work for you ... bringing you the needed relief to whatever situation, circumstance or problem you may be facing.

You might even say that **God is about to flex His muscles on your behalf.**

Exodus 6:6 in the Amplified Bible says:

"Accordingly, say to the Israelites, I am the Lord, and I will bring you out from under the burdens of the Egyptians, and I will free you from their bondage, and I will rescue you with an out-stretched arm [with special and vigorous action] and by mighty acts of judgment."

Are you hearing this? God will free you from bondage.

The Hebrew word for *bondage* is **abad** (H5647) and it means:

"to compel to labor or work, cause to labor, cause to serve; to cause to serve as subjects."

Debt, disease, depression, disappointment, despondency, discouragement ... all of these words represent bondage because they are used by the enemy to keep you living a meager existence ... never fulfilling your God-inspired and -created potential for success.

This type of bondage will never cause you to rise to any challenge. You will always acquiesce to the lowest standard … feeling that you're not worthy of success or even to taste His precious promises for your life.

But God … I love saying that … BUT GOD … is about to turn things around for you and free you from bondage.

Jeremiah 32:17 says:

"… there is nothing too hard for thee."

According to Strong's Concordance the word *nothing* is the Hebrew word ***dabar*** (H1697) which means:

"speech, word, deed, business, act."

There is no word that needs to be spoken … no deed that needs to be done and no act that has to be performed … that is too hard for God to make happen on your behalf.

Nothing or "no thing" is too hard for God to speak and flex His muscles on your behalf.

Now if that doesn't get you excited and confident in the Word … you are definitely suffering from rigor mortis of the mind.

God not only wants you to "see" it … He wants you to experience it!

Not only is God going to speak and act on your behalf,

but a close examination shows that the word *hard* ... as in "nothing is too hard for thee" ... is the Hebrew word **pala** (H6381) which means:

"to be marvelous, be wonderful, be surpassing, be extraordinary, separate by distinguishing action; to be beyond one's power, be difficult to do."

Not only is God going to speak and work on your behalf ... He is going to do wonderful, extraordinary, and marvelous things for you.

No matter what you're facing ... no matter how big the giant ... no matter how severe the financial drought and economic famine may be ... there is only one thing you need to know ... your Heavenly Father is ready to speak and flex His powerful muscles on your behalf.

How do you spell relief from whatever tricks, traps, lies and deceptions the enemy throws your way ... it's simple: G O D ... that's how you spell relief, and when He moves on your behalf ... you're going to say, "Ah, Lord God," ... I needed that.

Think about these scriptures ... get them down in your spirit.

Exodus 23:22 says:

"But if you will indeed listen to and obey His voice ... I will be an enemy to your enemies and

an adversary to your adversaries."

Personalize this ... Ilene ... LeJune ... Derek ...

"But if [Name] will indeed listen to and obey His voice ... I will be an enemy to your enemies and an adversary to your adversaries."

Yvonne ... Paul ... Steph ...

Joshua 21:45 in The Living Bible is GOING TO MAKE YOU SHOUT. It says:

"Every good thing the Lord promised them came true."

Personalize this:

"Every good thing the Lord promised [Name] came true."

Janine ... Jean-Marie ... Denise ...

Romans 8:31 in the Amplified Bible says:

"... if God is for us, who [can be] against us? [Who can be our foe, if God is on our side?]"

Personalize this:

"... if God is for [Name], who [can be] against [Name]? [Who can be [Name]'s foe, if God is on [his/her] side?]"

God will deliver you from the slavery of debt and lack.

2 Chronicles 20:27 in the Message Bible says:

> *"... God had given them joyful relief from their enemies! ..."*

With God speaking and working on your behalf ... every enemy of the God who lives within you will be destroyed.

Can somebody say Hallelujah!!!!!!

Day 9

Success, or Just Getting By

Would you like to be known as a successful person, or as someone who just gets by?

Would you like to meet and socialize with important people? And by the way, there is a difference between important and successful people.

Seem impossible to you? It's not ... according to the Word of God, specifically Proverbs 22:29:

"Seest thou a man diligent in his business? he shall stand before kings; he shall not stand before mean men."

The key to meeting, working and socializing with important people is to be "diligent" in your business.

It's important to understand that being diligent in your business does not necessarily mean that you have to own your own business.

The word *diligent* is the Hebrew word **mahiyr** (H4106) which means:

"quick, prompt, skilled, ready."

The Message Bible translation of Proverbs 22:29 says:

"Observe people who are good at their work—skilled workers are always in demand and admired; they don't take a backseat to anyone."

Sam Walton, the founder of Wal-Mart, said:

"If you love your work, you'll be out there every day trying to do it the best you possibly can and pretty soon everybody around will catch the passion from you—like a fever."

Yes, but Brother Harold, that's hard, because you don't know the kind of people I work for.

That may be true, but God does.

Ephesians 6:7 says:

"With good will doing service, as to the Lord, and not to men."

God anticipated you'd run into this problem and gave you an answer to it. Getting a fresh revelation of this scripture will change a person's attitude and work ethic.

When you understand the principle of performing your assigned responsibilities as unto the Lord and not to men, <u>you immediately add an extra dimension of powerful success and advancement to whatever vocation you might be involved in</u>.

This mindset will immediately increase the value you place on the things that you do for your employer. At the same time, your position of employment will take on a much higher level of value.

There is a powerful principle of increase behind the mindset of being the Lord's employee.

If you're doing your job as unto the Lord, there will be a more valuable standard of excellence that will guide your effectiveness as well as your enthusiasm for your job.

Not long ago it was popular to wear a bracelet that said, "WWJD" (What Would Jesus Do?). That is the same question you must answer every day on your job. **<u>What would you do differently on your job if you knew that Jesus would be evaluating your performance</u>?**

Truthfully, He is. The scripture is quite clear. We should do "EVERYTHING" as unto the Lord.

How do you increase your effectiveness so you can be classified as diligent?

Proverbs 1:5 says:

"A wise man will hear; and will increase learn-ing."

Paul wrote to young Timothy in 1 Timothy 4:13:

"… give attendance to reading …"

Then in 2 Timothy 2:15, he said:

"Study to show thyself approved … a workman that needeth not to be ashamed …"

Hosea in Hosea 4:6 proclaimed:

"My people are destroyed (bound) for a lack of knowledge."

It is interesting that Hosea did not say that Satan would destroy you. He says that ignorance would destroy you. Satan just helps you enjoy staying ignorant.

Write this down …

> **TODAY is the last day … I'll ever be ignorant about anything.**

The right information will not only promote you, it will motivate you and give you confidence.

Proverbs 11:9 says:

"... through knowledge shall the just be delivered."

The difference between success and just getting by is usually due to three forces.

1. Information

The successful person knows something that others have not yet discovered or cared to pursue. They **find time to enjoy good books or audio/video teachings that will prepare and provoke them to stretch beyond their previous level of achievement**. This works for successful people, and it will most surely WORK FOR YOU.

Let me ask you a question ...

With a new passion for acquiring knowledge, what books and audio/video teachings should be on your priority list? May I humbly suggest ... everything in the Debt Free Army store ... through the words in this book ... can you sense the smile on my face?

2. Motivation

You must start clearly defining projects and goals that lie before you. **See to it that you work with real**

enthusiasm in whatever you're doing.

Here are two Power Thoughts to help you understand more clearly what enthusiasm really means. Now I've shared this before … but I will do it again and again … until we get it.

First, the last four letters of the word "enthusi- asm" are "-iasm" which stand for "I am sold my- self." You must commit to believing in what you do— God will help it not be "grievous" to you if you commit it to Him.

Second, the word "enthusiasm" literally means "God within." When we can allow the greater one within us to stir our greatest desire for excellence, we will have all the motivation we need.

What is your motivation? What are your projects and goals? Be specific.

Zig Ziglar said:

> **"Every job is a self-portrait of the person who did it."**

3. Associations

<u>A successful person knows how to build a bridge in- stead of a barrier</u>. **You're influenced by who you associate with**. Make it a blessing.

Spend your time with those who can encourage, edify, lift you up, build you up and sincerely want you to be all that God created you to be.

In Genesis 39:5, in the English Standard Version, the scripture says:

> *"... the LORD blessed the Egyptian's [Potipher's] house for Joseph's sake."*

In Genesis 30:27, Laban said to Jacob:

> *"... I have learned by experience that God blessed me for your sake."*

Spend your time with people who can challenge you to even greater levels of accomplishment.

Create a list of people with whom you like to associate and why.

If you are caught in a position where you must be the Joseph or Jacob on your job, then rely on God to make you the example just as they were to Potiphar and Laban. **The Holy Spirit will bring you out with a high hand … can somebody say Hallelujah!**

Now create a list of people that you would like to be associated with, people who can help you get where God wants you to be on your job.

Now I want to give you several other important scriptural reasons why diligence will lead to your personal growth and success.

First, a diligent work ethic is essential ... being lazy just doesn't cut it.

Proverbs 10:4 says:

> *"He becometh poor that dealeth with a slack hand: but the hand of the diligent maketh rich."*

The New Living Translation of Proverbs 10:4 says:

> *"Lazy people are soon poor; hard workers get rich."*

Being diligent will also determine your freedom ... financial and otherwise.

Proverbs 12:24 in the New Living Translation says:

> *"Work hard and become a leader; be lazy and become a slave."*

The Message Bible translation of Proverbs 12:24 adds another dimension of clarity to this scripture:

> *"The diligent find freedom in their work; the lazy are oppressed by work."*

Second, a diligent person will plan their work and work their plan.

Proverbs 21:5 says:

> *"The thoughts of the diligent tend only to plenteousness; but of every one that is hasty only to want."*

The New Living Translation of Proverbs 21:5 says:

> *"Good planning and hard work lead to prosperity, but hasty shortcuts lead to poverty."*

So, if you're diligent in your business … whether working for yourself or others … the words of Proverbs 27:23 will take on extra meaning in your life.

> *"Be thou diligent to know the state of thy flocks, and look well to thy herds."*

The scriptures are clear … **if you're diligent … the first important and successful person you meet each day will be the one you look at in a mirror.**

Day 10

What Makes a Man Good?

Each May we celebrate Mother's Day ... and many Moms are blessed by Mother's Day cards ... it's estimated by Hallmark that over 141 million cards are exchanged each year along with other meaningful gifts, and that's wonderful.

However, the best gift any son could give his mother, or any husband can give his wife ... is to be a good man.

Let's talk about 14 things that make a man ... good.

Is a man good ... because he's **faithfully worked for the same company for twenty years?**

Is a man good ... because he's been good to his spouse and children?

Is a man good ... because he **coached kids' sports programs?**

Is a man good ... because he or someone says so?

If your **favorite high-profile preacher says someone is a good man** ... that means one thing.

When Don Corlene, the Godfather, says his **favorite hit man is a good man ... that's something else.**

A terrorist may think a **man is good because he carries out a suicide mission that kills hundreds of innocent people.**

A military officer may think a man is good **because he fell on an incoming grenade to save the lives of fellow soldiers in his platoon.**

Determining whether a man is good or not is most often in the eye of the beholder. However, there are **ways you can tell whether or not someone is a good man regardless of who's making the observations.**

How? Well ... how does the Word of God define a good man?

1. Sharing the good news ...

1 Kings 1:42 in the New Living Translation says:

*"... for you are a **good man**. You must have good news."*

2. Seeking divine direction for every step you take ...

Psalm 37:23 says:

*"The steps of a **good man** are ordered by the*

Lord: and he delighteth in his way."

3. Giving favor and blessing others …

The first part of Psalm 112:5 says:

*"A **good man** sheweth favour, and lendeth …"*

4. Conducting your business with integrity …

The last part of Psalm 112:5 says:

*"A **good man** … will guide his affairs with discretion."*

5. Leaving an inheritance to your grandchildren …

Proverbs 13:22 says:

*"A **good man** leaveth an inheritance to his children's children: and the wealth of the sinner is laid up for the just."*

6. Receiving a reward for righteous living …

Proverbs 14:14 in the New Living Translation says:

*"Backsliders get what they deserve; **good people** receive their reward."*

7. Earning respect in your community …

Genesis 6:9 in the Message Bible says:

*"This is the story of Noah: Noah was a **good man**, a man of integrity in his community. Noah walked with God."*

8. Living in prayerful expectation ...

Luke 2:25 in the Message Bible says:

*"In Jerusalem at the time, there was a man, Simeon by name, a **good man**, a man who lived in the prayerful expectancy of help for Israel. And the Holy Spirit was on him. The Holy Spirit had shown him that he would see the Messiah of God before he died."*

9. Speaking the Word that's stored in your heart ...

Matthew 12:35 says:

*"A **good man** out of the good treasure of the heart bringeth forth good things: and an evil man out of the evil treasure bringeth forth evil things."*

Luke 6:45 says:

*"A **good man** out of the good treasure of his heart bringeth forth that which is good; and an evil man out of the evil treasure of his heart bringeth forth that which is evil: for of the abundance of the heart his mouth speaketh."*

10. Being filled with the Holy Ghost and full of faith …

Acts 11:24 says:

*"For he was a **good man**, and full of the Holy Ghost and of faith: and much people was added unto the Lord."*

11. Leading people to worship the Lord …

Acts 10:1-2 in the Message Bible says:

*"There was a man named Cornelius who lived in Caesarea, captain of the Italian Guard stationed there. He was a thoroughly **good man**. He had led everyone in his house to live worshipfully before God, was always helping people in need, and had the habit of prayer."*

12. Living a life that will cause your deliverance from wickedness …

2 Peter 2:7 in the New Living Translation says:

*"But at the same time, God rescued Lot out of Sodom because he was a **good man** who was sick of all the immorality and wickedness around him."*

13. Confidence in who you are in Christ … makes you a good man.

Acts 11:22 in the Message Bible says:

"When the church in Jerusalem got wind of this, they sent Barnabas to Antioch to check on things. As soon as he arrived, he saw that God was behind and in it all.

*"He threw himself in with them, got behind them, urging them to stay with it the rest of their lives. He was a **good man** that way, enthusiastic and confident in the Holy Spirit's ways. The community grew large and strong in the Master."*

14. A good man would rather have the favor of the Lord than anything else.

Proverbs 12:2 says:

*"A **good man** obtaineth favour of the Lord: but a man of wicked devices will he condemn."*

There's more to being a good man **than just having someone say that you are one.**

"You're a good man, Charlie Brown." Charles Schultz

Without question Charlie Brown had to be a **good man to put up with the antics of Lucy.**

I enjoy the *Peanuts* comic strip because it teaches principles with humor.

When principles aren't taught ... where Godly

influences don't exist in the lives of children … <u>trouble follows</u>.

I came across a profound quote, but I'm not sure who said it.

"A good man dies when a boy goes wrong." Anonymous

But it doesn't have to be that way … more properly, **God doesn't want it to be that way.**

Either get involved with the children and youth at your church, or financially invest in their future. **It will pay great dividends.**

Edmund Burke said: "All that is necessary for evil to triumph is for good men to do nothing."

That's why you **can't be a spectator in the game of life. Sitting in the bleachers cheering or complaining about the ways things are … won't change a thing except your spiritual, mental and physical health.** All three will get worse.

"The blues ain't nothing but a good man feelin' bad." Leon Redbone

When you've got the Word of God in you … **when you're practicing the 14 qualities of a good man that the Bible lists**, then you "ain't gonna be feeling bad."

I came across a quote from one of my favorite actors and directors, Clint Eastwood. In one of his movies he made the following statement.

"A good man always knows his limitations."

Child of God, **as a born-again, spirit-filled believer, we can experience no limitations,** because the Word of God says so.

Luke 1:37 in the Amplified Bible says:

*"For with God nothing is ever impossible **and no word from God shall be without power or impossible of fulfillment."***

When a good man moves with full knowledge and is full of the Word, he is without limitation.

Matthew 17:20 in the Amplified Bible says:

*"... For truly I say to you, if you have faith [that is living] like a grain of mustard seed, you can say to this mountain, Move from here to yonder place, and it will move; and **nothing will be impossible to you."***

I came across an anonymous proverb that sums up why you should be a good man.

"Make yourself a good man, and then you can be certain there is at least one less skunk in the

world."

Finally, Marcus Aurelius said:

"Waste no more time arguing about what a good man should be. Be one."

How can you become a good man?

Seven words: **READ YOUR BIBLE** ... **DO WHAT IT SAYS**.

Hear It! Read It! Live It! Love it! Manifest It!

Day 11

I Will Make You Rich

I believe there are times when God allows us to see one thing in the scriptures so He can show us something else.

Isaiah 1:19 says:

"If ye be willing and obedient, ye shall eat the good of the land."

So I've read and taught Isaiah 1:19 many times. However, I will always remember the day when I first felt stirred to read that verse in something other than the King James Version of the Bible. I read it in 8 translations, but the 9th one got my attention.

Isaiah 1:19 in The Living Bible says:

"If you will only let me help you, if you will only obey, then I will make you rich!"

Needless to say, I got excited by that translation … but it was vastly different from the other eight … or so I thought at first glance.

Then I was reminded how in biblical times the wealth, success and wisdom of a person was often judged by the type of feast they prepared.

The Lord brought to my remembrance the encounter between the Queen of Sheba and King Solomon.

In 1 Kings 10:4-5, the Amplified Bible says:

"When the queen of Sheba had seen all Solomon's wisdom and skill, the house he had built, the food of his table, the seating of his officials, the standing at attention of his servants, their apparel, his cupbearers, his ascent by which he went up to the house of the Lord [or the burnt offerings he sacrificed], she was breathless and overcome."

I personally believe there is great and eternal significance where every word is placed in the scriptures. I realize there are those who might disagree, and that is their prerogative ... when we all get to heaven ... we can get the final revelation on the subject.

In this scripture, *"the food of his table"* ranks right after King Solomon's wisdom and the house that he built for the Lord.

A man's wealth and wisdom were judged by the presentation, variety, quality and quantity of the food he served.

When the Prodigal Son returned home … his father treated him with a great feast.

There are numerous examples of how great events were celebrated with feasts or how people ate the "good of the land."

As I meditated on the "good of the land," several questions came to my mind.

First, whose land are we talking about? If the people are feasting off the good of their land … that obviously makes them landowners. In biblical times, if you owned land … it was a sign of wealth.

Basically, there was no middle class at the time … so a person was either rich or poor.

Second, if you were feasting off somebody else's land, then you were a person of significance. A person to whom honor and respect was given. The kind of person for whom, like the Queen of Sheba, feasts were thrown in your honor.

Needless to say, <u>rich people would not have thrown a feast for a poor person or one of insignificance</u>.

So the only conclusion is that the person who is eating the "good of the land" was either a wealthy landowner or an important person who was shown honor because of his or her position in life.

I do think the matters we've been discussing up to this

point are of the greatest importance when looking at Isaiah 1:19.

First, the King James Version says: *"If you are willing and obedient ..."*

This is where things became a little more interesting.

The Hebrew word for *willing* is **'abah** (H14) and it means:

"to be willing, consent, desire."

In other words, it means "if you agree to" or "if your desire is to do this."

The Hebrew word for *obedient* is **shama`** (H8085) and it means:

"to hear, listen to, obey."

It is significant that *shama`* is found 1161 times in 1072 verses in the Hebrew Concordance of the King James Bible.

In 786 uses of *shama`* it is translated as the word **"hear."** It is also translated as "hearken" on 196 occasions, and as "obey" on 81 occasions.

In essence, the verse is saying, <u>**if you desire to hear what I'm saying ... then you will enjoy the good of the land**</u>.

The Living Bible says: *"If you will only let me help you, if you will only obey …"*

When does God help us? The answer is simple: when we desire to listen to what He has to say and follow His instructions.

This is further evidenced by Isaiah 1:20 in The Living Bible which says:

> *"But if you keep on turning your backs and refusing to listen to me, you will be killed by your enemies; I, the Lord, have spoken."*

I'm not talking about the "-ites" the children of Israel had to face … I'm talking about the enemies you have to deal with every day … debt, sickness, lack, depression. These enemies will kill you just as quickly as the arrows, spears or bullets of a natural enemy.

Do you get that? **We suffer the consequences of death and defeat when we refuse to listen to our Heavenly Father.**

What will allow us to eat the good of the land and become rich? Having an insatiable desire to listen to Him … to follow His instructions.

2 Timothy 3:16-17 says:

> *"All scripture is given by inspiration of God, and is profitable for doctrine, for reproof, for*

correction, for instruction in righteousness: That the man of God may be perfect, thoroughly furnished unto all good works."

If something is profitable … it's going to be beneficial. <u>The word *profitable* in the Strong's Concordance is from a Greek word that means "profitable, advantage."</u>

Seven words come to mind. READ YOUR BIBLE … DO WHAT IT SAYS.

In Isaiah 1:19 in The Living Bible it says:

"If you will only let me help you, if you will only obey, then I will make you rich!"

When the scripture says, "If you will only let me help you, if you will only obey …" it clearly means we have a choice.

We can choose to follow God's instructions and reap the benefit … that's the obviously smart choice.

Or we can ignore God's instructions and suffer the consequences … plainly spoken, that's the "D & S" (dumb and stupid) response.

As I was typing these words, the Lord also brought to mind 2 Chronicles 26:5 which in the Amplified Bible says:

"He set himself to seek God in the days of

Zechariah, who instructed him in the things of God; and as long as he sought (inquired of, yearned for) the Lord, God made him prosper."

The word *"prosper"* according to the Strong's Concordance is the Hebrew word **tsalach** (H6743) which means:

"to make prosperous, bring to successful issue, cause to prosper."

What will cause you to be prosperous, successful and rich … to seek and yearn for the wisdom of the Lord … to hear His voice?

Job 36:11 says:

"If they obey and serve him, they shall spend their days in prosperity, and their years in pleasures."

Personalize this verse with your name:

"If [Name] obeys and serves him, [Name] shall spend [his/her] days in prosperity, and [his/her] years in pleasures."

By the way, the word *obey* in Job 36:11 is exactly the same Hebrew word for the word *obedient* found in Isaiah 1:19. As a reminder, it means "to hear."

Consider the Message Bible translation of Job 36:11:

"If they obey and serve him, they'll have a good, long life on easy street."

If you want a long, good life ... where you are rich, eat the good of the land and live on easy street ... then *it would be scripturally wise to willingly hear and obey God's voice and His instructions for living.*

Here is an email from Beverly in Austin, Texas, lifting up the renewing power of the Almighty God:

"I praise God for you and the anointing God has given you to minister to His people!

"Thank you so much for the Spiritual Entrepreneur. It has blessed me more than you will ever know. God bless you and your fine wife, Bev, and your family to thousands of generations! I expect God's best for myself, my children, my grandchildren, and my family! In the spiritual, relational, emotional, physical and mental areas of our lives, I take the limits off of God!"

Day 12

Secrets Revealed and Rewarded

Do you want to know a secret?

Do you promise not to tell?

Does that sound like the words of a Beatles song, or questions that have been asked and answered ... sometimes truthfully and sometimes not?

Isaiah 48:6-8 in the New Living Translation says:

> *"You have heard my predictions and seen them fulfilled, but you refuse to admit it. Now I will tell you new things, secrets you have not yet heard. They are brand new, not things from the past. So you cannot say, 'We knew that all the time!' Yes, I will tell you of things that are entirely new, things you never heard of before ..."*

Hallelujah!!

The Message Bible translation of Isaiah 48:6-7 says:

> *"This is new, brand-new, something you'd never*

guess or dream up. When you hear this you won't be able to say, 'I knew that all along' ..."

A secret is something you've never known before ... something you've never heard of. Here are eight keys to having secrets revealed and rewarded.

1. Delight yourself in the Lord.

Every good and glorious gift and thing in our lives begins when we delight ourselves in the Lord. Peace, prosperity, provision, promotion and protection all come from delighting ourselves in the Lord.

As if that's not enough ... Psalm 37:4 reveals even more when it says:

"Delight yourself also in the Lord, and He will give you the desires and secret petitions of your heart."

He will give you ... *the desires and secret petitions of your heart.*

2. He will give you whatever you request.

Psalm 37:4 says:

"... He will give you the desires and secret petitions of your heart."

According to Strong's Concordance the Hebrew word for *desires* is **mish'alah** and it means:

"request, petition, desire."

The desire of my heart is to walk in financial independence so I can bless who I want, when I want, with as much as I want and for as long as I want. Of course, my blessings to others should be led by the Holy Ghost.

That's my request … my desire … what's yours?

Have you written it down … if not, as my fine wife, Bev, who's at my side as I write, says:

"You haven't missed your opportunity."

3. He knows everything about you.

You can keep secrets, at least for a while, from your spouse, your parents, your children, your friends, your employer and even your pastor … but **you can NEVER EVER keep anything secret from God.**

Psalm 38:9 in the Contemporary English Version says:

"You, Lord, know every one of my deepest desires, and my noisy groans are no secret to you."

Jeremiah 17:10 in the New International Version says:

"I, the LORD, search the heart and examine the mind …"

We CAN'T keep secrets from God. He will examine our minds revealing what we're really thinking and what we've done.

Psalm 44:21 in the Contemporary English Version says:

"You would have known it because you discover every secret thought."

You need to know that your every secret thought ... is not secret.

4. Look what the Lord has done.

We should be continually praising God for what He has done and is doing in and through our lives.

Psalm 78:4 in the Contemporary English Version says:

"And we will tell them to the next generation. We won't keep secret the glorious deeds and the mighty miracles of the LORD."

If you need the supernatural intervention of God in your life ... praise Him for what He's already done for you.

5. God will expose anything done in secret against you.

If someone is saying bad things about you ... telling

untruths to your friends, supervisors or anyone else … embrace the promise found in Psalm 91:3 in the Contemporary English Version which says:

"The Lord will keep you safe from secret traps and deadly diseases."

> **You can trust that God will expose and punish those who plot evil against you.**

Ecclesiastes 12:14 in the Contemporary English Version says:

"God will judge everything we do, even what is done in secret, whether good or bad."

6. Your rewards will be God's recognition.

Isaiah 45:3 in the Contemporary English Version says:

"I will give you treasures hidden in dark and secret places. Then you will know that I, the LORD God of Israel, have called you by name."

Personalize this with your name … Steph … Trent … Rudy … Sarah …

"I will give [Name] treasures hidden in dark and secret places. Then [Name] will know that I, the LORD God of Israel, have called [him/her] by name."

Now, that scripture excites me on several levels. First, He's going to give me treasures ... second, and I might add, more importantly, He's calling me by name. Hallelujah!!

Jeremiah 17:10 in the New Living Translation says:

"But I, the Lord, search all hearts and examine secret motives. I give all people their due rewards, according to what their actions deserve."

It's important to understand that He will give you what your actions deserve ... and it can either be good or bad ... you determine the kind of reward you will receive.

Matthew 6:4 in the Contemporary English Version says:

"Then your gift will be given in secret. Your Father knows what is done in secret, and he will reward you."

I'd much rather God know about my generosity to others than anyone else I know. I'd rather have His reward than the accolades of any man.

7. God's recognition and rewards for you will happen.

Psalm 37:4 says:

"Delight yourself also in the Lord, and He will

give you the desires and secret petitions of your heart."

If you do this … delight yourself in the Lord … then He will give you the desires and wishes of your heart. It's not a maybe … He will … it's a done deal.

8. He will give you success.

Delighting yourself in the Lord will ensure your success in life. It's just that simple.

Psalm 20:4 in the New Living Translation says:

"May he grant your heart's desires and make all your plans succeed."

Personalize this with your name:

"May he grant [Name]'s heart's desires and make all [his/her/their] plans succeed."

One final thing to remember …

Delighting yourself in the Lord should never be a secret from Him or anyone else.

Abraham Lincoln famously said:

"No man is poor who has a godly mother."

He also said:

"I remember my mother's prayers and they have always followed me. They have clung to me all my life."

A Jewish proverb tells us:

"God could not be everywhere and therefore he made mothers."

Here are four humorous excerpts from the *Top Ten Things My Mother Taught Me*:

My mother taught me about **RELIGION:**

"You'd better pray that will come out of the carpet."

My mother taught me about **WEATHER:**

"This room of yours looks as if a tornado went through it."

My mother taught me about **HYPOCRISY:**

"If I told you once, I've told you a million times. Don't exaggerate!"

My mother taught me about **RECEIVING:**

"You are going to get it when you get home!"

First, if your Mom is still living, call her on Mother's Day regardless of what your relationship has been in the past.

If your Mom never exhibited Godly qualities, if she made mistakes in the past ... don't you make one. Call her on Mother's Day. You can't control what she does or has done, but you can control how the Christ in you would react.

Jesus always forgave ... how many times? Seven times seventy. Should you do any less?

Day 13

Visualization and Determination

Today … is a great day … in fact, the best day you'll ever have … to take charge of your destiny.

Today … is a great day … in fact, the best day you'll ever have … to plan your future.

No excuses … no ifs, ands or buts. This will be your day … your turning point … if you visualize and determine to make it so.

Visualization and Determination are key ingredients to your future success.

First, let's discuss visualization. We have allowed the New Age people to co-opt a term that is scripturally significant.

Romans 4:17 in the Amplified Bible says:

> *"As it is written, I have made you the father of many nations. [He was appointed our father] in*

the sight of God in Whom he believed, <u>Who</u> *<u>gives life to the dead and speaks of the nonex-</u>* *<u>istent things that [He has foretold and promised]</u>* *<u>as if they [already] existed</u>."*

The power of God allows us to ignite our imaginations and visualize His best ... His will ... for our lives.

Hebrews 11:1 says:

"Now faith is the substance of things hoped for, the evidence of things not seen."

This scripture confirms that everything will exist in the invisible realm before it can appear in the visible realm.

The phone you use to listen to a call was first visualized by someone before it was ever created.

The chair you are sitting in ... was visualized by someone before it was ever created and produced.

The cup you're drinking coffee from ... the paper you're writing notes on ... were invisible before someone visualized them ... coming into existence.

Every building that has ever existed or now exists on planet earth existed in the imagination of the builder or architect long before it existed in the visible realm.

Every process, every product, every invention, every

movie or entertainment vehicle, every book, every organization, everything that is added to the earth by mankind exists in the invisible realm of the imagination before it can enter the visible, tangible realm.

Allow your spirit to take hold of this truth.

I encourage you to allow natural information to stimulate your revelatory understanding.

When you visualize something, you are giving substance to the things that you are hoping for.

Let me give you an example that may help you visualize what I'm talking about.

A series of new Star Trek movies recently arrived in theaters around the world.

In Star Trek movies (and in the original television series) … the spaceship Enterprise was equipped with all the latest electronic gizmos including what they called the "transporter."

This electronic marvel is used to transport people and things from one part of the universe to the other. It dematerializes a person or object in one place and rematerializes them or it in another location.

People can be moved immediately from a place of danger to safety.

It should be noted that the "transporter" doesn't

discriminate between good and evil. There have been times when evil people and things were inadvertently transported during an episode or in part of the movies.

Through your imagination ... your ability to visualize an event, thing or the future becomes nothing more than a transporter.

This God-given ability (your imagination, serving as a mental transporter), when operated properly and in accordance with God's instructions, can bring the invisible things of God one step closer to the realm of the visible.

> **Like the transporter, the things that you visualize can either be good or evil.**

That's why 2 Corinthians 10:5 is so important. It says:

"Casting down imaginations, and every high thing that exalteth itself against the knowledge of God, and bringing into captivity every thought to the obedience of Christ."

It's imperative that you visualize the pure, the powerful and the positive from the Word of God. Each of us would do well to remember the words of Psalm 94:11 which say:

"The Lord knows the thoughts of man ..."

Here are seven things you need to be visualizing in your future.

1. A more intimate relationship with your Heavenly Father.

2. A closer relationship with your spouse, parents, children and/or friends.

3. Expanding your mental thought process through books, CDs, seminars, and most importantly, a mentor who can speak into your life.

4. Visualizing, expecting and manifesting supernatural connections and divine appointments.

5. How you will act and what you will do when you're totally, completely debt free.

6. How you can discover previously unknown opportunities in your life while tapping into your previously unused potential for success.

7. On a daily basis, visualize all that God has promised and provisioned for you.

> **Visualization without determination will never result in success or the supernatural manifestation you desire.**

<u>Your determination must come from God</u>.

Jeremiah 10:23 in the Amplified Bible says:

> *"O Lord [pleads Jeremiah in the name of the people], I know that [the determination of] the way of a man is not in himself; it is not in man [even in a strong man or in a man at his best] to direct his [own] steps."*

If God is determined to have you move in a certain direction at a certain time, then I suggest you follow it without hesitation or reservation, because He has a reason.

Consider the words found in the Message Bible translation of Genesis 41:28:

> *"The meaning is what I said earlier: God is letting Pharaoh in on what he is going to do. Seven years of plenty are on their way throughout Egypt. But on their heels will come seven years of famine, leaving no trace of the Egyptian plenty. As the country is emptied by famine, there won't be even a scrap left of the previous plenty—the famine will be total. The fact that Pharaoh dreamed the same dream twice emphasizes <u>God's determination</u> to do this and do it soon."*

Determination is so important ... because the enemy will use every trick, trap, lie, deception and wile at his disposal to keep you from achieving the things that God has allowed you to visualize for your future.

If you're doing anything remotely productive for the Kingdom of God ... the enemy is going to attempt to render you ineffective ... short-circuit your plans and create doubt about your ability to manifest what God has allowed you to visualize.

Don't be discouraged by others.

Nehemiah 6:9 in the New Living Translation says:

> *"They were just trying to intimidate us, imagining that they could discourage us and stop the work. So I continued the work with even greater determination."*

> As you bring about the manifestation of what God has allowed you to see, **make sure you never lose sight of your first priority.**

1 Corinthians 2:2 says:

> *"For I determined not to know anything among you, save Jesus Christ, and him crucified."*

It's important we adhere to the words found in Psalm 17:3 in the New Living Translation which says:

> *"You have tested my thoughts and examined my heart in the night. You have scrutinized me and*

found nothing wrong. I am <u>determined</u> not to sin in what I say."

Psalm 119:30 in the New Living Translation says:

"I have chosen to be faithful; I have <u>determined</u> to live by your regulations."

The necessity of a determined effort to obey His instructions is further confirmed a little later in Psalm 119, where Verse 112 in the New Living Translation says:

"I am <u>determined</u> to keep your decrees to the very end."

Beyond the scriptures that I've given you ... I want to share with you two of my favorite quotations on determination.

Someone once said: **"Determination today leads to success tomorrow."**

Tommy LaSorda, the long-time manager of the Los Angeles Dodgers, once said:

"The difference between the possible and the impossible lies in a person's determination."

Determination simply means ... a personal resolve to never give in, give up, back up, back down, quit or walk away until you've accomplished the thing that is set before you.

With visualization and determination you will be able to achieve all that God has written in your book of life ... plus you'll be able to share these powerful ideas with someone else.

Day 14

8 Things You Ought To Know About You

I have found over the years that if there is something we don't understand or haven't been able to manifest in our own life ... it's often easier to condemn it rather than discover what's hindering the manifestation.

Hopefully, with time, intelligence and insight, we will all overcome that immature way of thinking.

The reality is that way too many God-fearing, heaven-bound believers create an immediate and a progressive hindrance to their prosperity because of a **belief that only some people can be wealthy.**

As I was praying, the Lord allowed me to understand a little more fully why some people have a selective view of what God will and will not do for them.

If you come from a family with siblings ... did you ever feel that your mom, dad or both favored one brother or sister over you?

As a child, did you ever play any sports or games where teams were chosen? Two captains took turns picking members for their teams. Were you the first one chosen or perhaps the last?

In school, were you the teacher's pet, or was it someone else?

On your job, does someone else get the credit for work that you do? Do others seem to get all the promotions?

From an early age ... many people have a history of being overlooked, neglected or ignored. It seems like it is someone else who is always selected, honored, rewarded or appreciated.

Over the years, a certain type of mentality begins to be programmed into a person's mental hard drive ... one that causes them to think they will never be able to experience the best.

It may not even be true ... but the perception is enough to begin developing the mistaken idea of not being accepted.

One of our daughters had a friend who didn't like going to Awards Night at the end of the school year. Since she was close with our family, I remember my fine wife, Bev, calling her to urge her to attend. She said she didn't want to because she never got recognized anyway, yet she was a top-notch student.

We always made it a point to have our children attend so they could learn to support and be happy for others, even if they didn't get recognized themselves. That particular year, this girl's name was called out 4 or 5 times for different accolades, but she was not there to hear it.

She went on to receive a full Presidential Scholarship to college, but somehow she felt like all the awards went to others.

Sadly, this attitude can easily carry over to a person's walk as a Christian as well. To prevent that, it needs to be recognized and dealt with.

Acts 10:34 says:

"Then Peter opened his mouth, and said, Of a truth I perceive that God is no respecter of persons."

The New International Version says:

"Then Peter began to speak: 'I now realize how true it is that God does not show favoritism.' "

The Message Bible translation is even clearer:

"Peter fairly exploded with his good news: 'It's God's own truth, nothing could be plainer: God plays no favorites! It makes no difference who you are or where you're from—if you want God and are ready to do as he says, the door is open.' "

I've read Acts 10:34 in thirteen different translations, and I haven't seen any sort of asterisk or footnote indicating that this scripture doesn't apply to everybody on planet earth.

Once again, there are people who can quote this scripture but still doubt it, because they've accepted a misconception based on what has been programmed into their mental thought processes.

I was blessed as a child. From my earliest recollection, I always remember my parents telling me that I could do anything.

This positive reinforcement continued in the face of less than stellar grades.

> **The message all my life was that I could do anything I set my mind to do.**

In that regard, I was and continue to be blessed.

I have the distinction of being the youngest and oldest child in my family ... I'm it, the only child ... so I was always the favorite child.

Regardless of your background ... the Word of God becomes the great equalizer in how you view yourself.

That's why it's crucially important to begin to see yourself the way God sees you.

Let's take a moment and look at eight things the Word of God says about you.

First, YOU are the child of the most high God.

Genesis 1:26 in The Living Bible says:

> *"Then God said, 'Let us make a man—someone like ourselves, to be the master of all life upon the earth and in the skies and in the seas.' "*

Second, YOU are the head and not the tail.

Deuteronomy 28:13 in the New Living Translation says:

> *"If you listen to these commands of the Lord your God that I am giving you today, and if you carefully obey them, the Lord will make you the head and not the tail, and you will always be on top and never at the bottom."*

Third, YOU are above and not beneath.

Deuteronomy 28:13 in the King James Version says:

> *"… and thou shalt be above only, and thou shalt not be beneath; if that thou hearken unto the commandments of the LORD thy God, which I command thee this day, to observe and to do them."*

Fourth, YOU are a joint heir with Christ.

Romans 8:17 says:

> *"And if children, then heirs; heirs of God, and joint-heirs with Christ ..."*

Fifth, YOU are blessed in the city and blessed in the field.

Deuteronomy 28:3 says:

> *"Blessed shalt thou be in the city, and blessed shalt thou be in the field."*

Sixth, YOU are more than a conqueror.

Romans 8:37 says:

> *"Nay, in all these things we are more than conquerors through him that loved us."*

Seventh, YOU are guaranteed a harvest for whatever seed you sow.

Galatians 6:7 in the Amplified Bible says:

> *"Do not be deceived and deluded and misled; God will not allow Himself to be sneered at (scorned, disdained, or mocked by mere pretensions or professions, or by His precepts being set aside.) [He inevitably deludes himself who attempts to delude God.] <u>For whatever a man sows, that and that only is what he will reap.</u>"*

Eighth, YOU have the mind of Christ.

1 Corinthians 2:16 in the Amplified Bible says:

> "… *But we have the mind of Christ (the Messiah) and do hold the thoughts (feelings and purposes) of His heart.*"

Personalize this … Miya … Nicole … Jannine …

> "*But [Name] has the mind of Christ (the Messiah) and does hold the thoughts (feelings and purposes) of His heart.*"

These eight scriptures make it very clear that you are no different than any other believer who ever drew a breath on planet earth.

There is no reason to question God's promises to you, because He is not capable of telling a lie.

Numbers 23:19 in the Amplified Bible says:

> "*God is not a man, that He should tell or act a lie, neither the son of man, that He should feel repentance or compunction [for what He has promised]. Has He said and shall He not do it? Or has He spoken and shall He not make it good?*"

God doesn't lie, and He doesn't play favorites. He doesn't selectively apply His principles, promises, precepts and rewards to one person and not another.

ANYONE WHO WORKS THE WORD OF GOD WILL EVENTUALLY SEE THE FRUIT.

It is the devil that wants you to doubt whether or not God will bless you with biblical prosperity.

Your view of God's view of you ... will either open the floodgates of heaven or keep them closed tight.

You may never have had an earthly parent who believed in you ... but you have a Heavenly Father who certainly does.

Romans 12:6 in The Living Bible says:

"God has given each of us the ability to do certain things well ..."

If you don't what you can do well ... ASK ... God will show you.

7 Questions About the Word and World Economies

Here's a question or two for you ... are you currently manifesting biblical prosperity?

If not, why not?

It's clear that God wants you to prosper ... that's not my opinion ... it's all through the Word of God.

3 John 2 says:

> *"Beloved, I wish above all things that thou mayest prosper and be in health, even as thy soul prospereth."*

What's the holdup? What's the hindrance? Increased prosperity and good health hinge on your soul prospering, and that involves the Word of God.

One of the main hindrances is a lack of knowledge about what the Word of God says about the world and the Word economy.

<u>There is nothing wrong with lacking financial knowl-edge unless you have no motivation to increase your understanding.</u>

James 1:5 in the Amplified Bible says:

> *"If any of you is deficient in wisdom, let him ask of the giving God [Who gives] to everyone liber-ally and ungrudgingly, without reproaching or faultfinding, and it will be given him."*

The Message Bible translation of James 1:5 continues in Verse 6 by saying:

> *"... Ask boldly, believingly, without a second thought."*

Without a second thought ... no doubts. As the old saying goes, doubt and do without.

Without hesitation or reservation ... you've got to know God will give you revelation and access to everything you need to know in the financial arena.

Once you understand that everything you have be-longs to God ... that you are just a steward of His re-sources ... then you can begin to realize that God will hold you personally accountable on Judgment Day for how you've handled or mishandled His goods. When you catch this revelation ... you will begin to view money differently.

I'm feeling impressed right now … at this very moment … to tell you to remove all limitations to your thinking.

It stirred in me that there are people … who don't think they're smart enough to grasp financial principles … and that's a lie.

The enemy of your financial future will tell you that you'll never understand either the Word or the world economy. <u>He is a liar, the father of lies and the truth is not in him</u> (John 8:44).

Hosea 4:6 says:

> *"My people are destroyed for lack of knowledge: because thou hast rejected knowledge, I will also reject thee, that thou shalt be no priest to me: seeing thou hast forgotten the law of thy God, I will also forget thy children."*

The scripture doesn't say that we're destroyed by the devil … it says … we're destroyed by a lack of knowledge.

<u>The devil can't keep you down … but a lack of knowledge can</u>. Don't reject knowledge … God will reject you.

Open your mind and heart to receive what God wants to release into your life TODAY.

In order to determine your world and Word financial IQ (or knowledge), I'll ask you seven questions in these areas: (1) the world, (2) the Word.

Don't be discouraged if you don't know every answer ... the key is that you're willing to do what is necessary to increase your understanding.

Remember the words of Proverbs 1:5 in the Amplified Bible:

"The wise also will hear and increase in learning, and the person of understanding will acquire skill and attain to sound counsel [so that he may be able to steer his course rightly]."

Our first seven questions are about the world economy as it pertains to your financial future.

1. Do you know if your employer offers a 401K? If so, do you know if they will match or add to your contributions? If not, do you fully understand the options that are available to you individually?

2. Do you know your credit score?

3. Do you realize that getting a large income tax refund means that you've been allowing the government to use your money for free during the past year? Do you know what to do to stop that?

4. Do you know the best way to price-shop for a new or pre-owned car?

5. Do you know the exact amount of your total indebtedness?

6. Do you know how much surplus you have, if any, each month after all your bills are paid in full?

7. Do you have a plan to pay off all your debts rapidly?

There is no passing or failing grade with the seven questions I've just asked. They are designed to provoke your thinking and allow you to see areas where you could increase your wisdom and understanding.

Remember, <u>there's nothing wrong with not knowing, as long as you choose not to remain ignorant of your financial destiny</u>.

1 Corinthians 15:34 in the Amplified Bible says:

"... For some of you have not the knowledge of God [you are utterly and willfully and disgracefully ignorant, and continue to be so, lacking the sense of God's presence and all true knowledge of Him]. I say this to your shame."

Now, let's look at seven financial questions from the Word.

1. Do you believe that Jesus came to this earth so that you might have abundant life (now) and eternal life (later)? (John 10:10)

2. Do you realize that God takes pleasure in your prosperity? (Psalm 35:27)

3. Do you believe and practice giving tithes and offering? (Malachi 3:10)

4. Do you believe that God is a respecter of persons, or do you accept that what He's done for someone else, He'll do for you, also? (Acts 10:34)

5. Do you understand that everything you sow in life will return a harvest? (Galatians 6:7)

6. Do you understand that everything you've lost or that has been stolen from you can be returned seven-fold? (Proverbs 6:30, 31)

7. Do you know there is going to be an end-time wealth transfer, and those who have shown themselves faithful will be involved? (Proverbs 13:22)

Needless to say, I could go on with the questions ... but it's important for you to understand that every question I asked is a provision found in the Word. God wants you to increase in wisdom and stature.

How can I know such a thing with absolute certainty?

Consider these two verses. First, John 14:12 says:

"Verily, verily, I say unto you, He that believeth on me, the works that I do shall he do also; and greater works than these shall he do; because I go unto my Father."

Second, Luke 2:52 says:

"And Jesus increased in wisdom and stature, and in favour with God and man."

If He increased ... **just think how much more He wants us to increase in knowledge and understanding when it comes to money.**

Proverbs 4:7 in the Amplified Bible says:

"The beginning of Wisdom is: get Wisdom (skillful and godly Wisdom)! [For skillful and godly Wisdom is the principal thing.] And with all you have gotten, get understanding (discernment, comprehension, and interpretation)."

J. Paul Getty once said:

"Your money's only as good as what you do with it."

Let's look at the words of Hosea 4:6 again but this time in the Amplified Bible:

"My people are destroyed for lack of knowledge;

because you [the priestly nation] have rejected knowledge, I will also reject you that you shall be no priest to Me; seeing you have forgotten the law of your God, I will also forget your children."

Finally, I feel led to close this teaching with the words found in Proverbs 9:6 in the Message Bible:

"... Leave your impoverished confusion and live! Walk up the street to a life with meaning."

My final words: It's not what you don't know that matters ... but rather what you're willing to learn and put into practice.

Day 16

Your Answer Is on the Way

As I listen to your phone messages and read your letters and emails, God allows me to feel your hurts and see your hopes for a better tomorrow.

Some of you have wondered either on paper or in your heart when the promises of God will be manifested in your life.

<u>I know that delay tactics are a favorite deception of the enemy, because he seeks to trip us up by filling us with doubt</u>.

The enemy wants you to believe that salvation will never come to your family ... but that's not what the Word says.

The enemy wants you to believe that deliverance from debt will never manifest in your life ... but that's not what the Word says.

The enemy wants you to believe that your healing or that of your loved one will never manifest ... but that's not what the Word says.

The enemy wants you to think the job market is hopeless, and you'll never get another job ... but that's not what the Word says.

The enemy wants you to think that the Lord is not interested in your needs or in fulfilling the promises that He makes to each of us in the Word of God.

2 Peter 3:9 in the Amplified Bible says:

> *"The Lord does not delay and is not tardy or slow about what He promises, according to some people's conception of slowness, but He is long-suffering (extraordinarily patient) toward you, not desiring that any should perish, but that all should turn to repentance."*

This scripture is often quoted as a verse to give hope to those who believe for a loved one to be saved. However, I think there is much more at work in this verse.

"The Lord does not delay and is not tardy or slow about what He promises ..."

If you've been going through the fire ... if you feel like you've been to hell and back ... then you need to hold to the first part of this verse.

God does not delay ... but the enemy likes to see if

he can hinder the arrival of God's answer to the circumstances, situations and problems that you are facing.

Daniel 10:12-14 in the New Living Translation says:

*"Then he said, 'Don't be afraid, Daniel. Since the first day you began to pray for understanding and to humble yourself before your God, **your request has been heard in heaven. I have come in answer to your prayer.** But for twenty-one days the spirit prince of the kingdom of Persia blocked my way. Then Michael, one of the archangels, came to help me, and I left him there with the spirit prince of the kingdom of Persia. Now I am here to explain what will happen to your people in the future, **for this vision concerns a time yet to come.'** "*

The Amplified Bible translation of Daniel 10:12 says:

"… your words were heard, and I have come as a consequence of [and in response to] your words."

It's important for you to understand that God has heard your prayer … that your answer … your deliverance is on the way.

However, we must obey the Lord … follow His instructions … never doubt … because answers, direction and deliverance are coming.

Heed the words of Psalm 119:60 in the New Living Translation which say:

"I will hurry, without delay, to obey your commands."

> **Even though you've been waiting for an answer ... a manifestation ... don't give up, give in, back up, back down or quit expecting.**

As I was praying over this teaching, the Lord led me to the story of Simeon found in Luke 2:25-26.

*"And, behold, there was a man in Jerusalem, whose name was Simeon; and the same man was **just** and **devout**, **waiting for the consolation of Israel**: and **the Holy Ghost was upon him.** And it was revealed unto him by the Holy Ghost, that he <u>should not see death, before he had seen the Lord's Christ</u>."*

> **It's important that we never give up on the promises of God.**

Simeon had been given a promise by God, and he was holding onto it. He may have been young when he received the promise, and now he was old, yet he held onto the promise the Holy Ghost gave him.

If God said it or promised it in His Word, then it will come to pass. As Dr. Robert Schuller once said, "Delay does not mean denial."

There are several characteristics used to describe Simeon that we need to emulate in our lives.

First, he was *just*.

According to Strong's Concordance the word *just* is the Greek word ***dikaios*** (G1342) and it means:

"Upright, righteous, virtuous, keeping the commands of God."

The word *just* is found 81 times in 76 verses according to the Hebrew Concordance of the King James Bible. Interestingly enough, the word *dikaios* is also translated as *righteous* on 41 occasions.

A further definition of *just* prompts a powerful question for us. Strong's Concordance also says:

"... whose way of thinking, feeling, and acting is wholly conformed to the will of God."

How are we living our lives as we await the manifestation of His promises?

What are we thinking about? Talking about? Are we focusing more on the things of this world than on the Word of God?

Are we determined to stay full of faith ... nothing wavering ... no doubt ... resting on His Word?

We are the main character in the story of our lives ... is our performance based on the Word?

Secondly, Verse 25 says that Simeon was *devout*.

According to the Strong's Concordance, *devout* is only found three times in the New Testament. Devout is the Greek word *eulabēs* (G2126) and it means:

"... reverencing God, pious, religious."

Devout men often take stands of faith that are misunderstood ... sometimes in the midst of persecution.

In Acts 8:2, the scripture says that it was *devout* men who buried Stephen after he had been stoned to death by an angry mob. These men had such a commitment that it didn't matter to them who saw them burying Stephen. The scripture says they even went with "lamentation," or beating their chests in grief.

A devout person is not moved by circumstances or the opinions of others.

The scripture says Simeon was "... waiting for the consolation of Israel." He was "looking forward to, waiting for" the consolation of Israel.

In Strong's Concordance we learn that *consolation* is from the Greek noun *paraklesis* meaning "comfort or

140

consolation." It comes from the root word **parakaleo**, which is to "call to one's side" then "help, encourage, comfort."

Thirdly, "… the Holy Ghost was upon him."

Before Jesus' resurrection, the Holy Spirit was on the prophets of God … after His death, the Holy Spirit came to live within us.

If you've been waiting for some promises of God to be manifested in your life as I have, Simeon gives us a good example of what's expected of us while we wait.

> **We must be righteous, keep the commands of God, reverence God in the midst of adversity and anticipate the manifestation with the power of the Holy Spirit upon us.**

If God promised you something was going to happen … the question isn't whether or not He will keep His Word … the only question is how you and I obey His Word while awaiting the manifestation.

How we live our lives … can speed up or delay the manifestation … sometimes we just have to wait for the timing of God … but truly God is not a man that He should lie. He will perform His Word.

Delay doesn't mean denial. Your answer is on the way.

If you hold fast to these three characteristics, then, like Simeon, your eyes will see the deliverance the Lord brings come into your life.

It's important for each of us to realize that our answer is on the way ... what we've been praying for ... believing for ... confessing ... the answer we seek is on the way.

And while you're waiting ... take comfort ... gain strength from Psalm 34:19 in the New Century Version which says:

"People who do what is right may have many problems, but the Lord will solve them all."

Why Are You Sleeping With the Frogs?

The only frog that I really like is Kermit the Frog.

A few years ago I did a meeting in Greenwood, South Carolina. As you drive into the city, there is a sign that says:

"Greenwood, Home of Kermit the Frog"

But today I'm not talking about Kermit; instead I'm interested in the frogs found in Exodus 8:1-4 in the Amplified Bible which says:

"Then the Lord said to Moses, Go to Pharaoh and say to him, Thus says the Lord, Let My people go, that they may serve Me. And if you refuse to let them go, behold, I will smite your entire land with frogs; And the river shall swarm with frogs which shall go up and come into your house, into your bedchamber and on your bed, and into the houses of your servants and upon your people, and into your ovens, your kneading bowls, and your dough. And the frogs shall

143

come up on you and on your people and all your servants."

Sometimes we run into frogs. But can you imagine having frogs everywhere in your house ... you settle down for a peaceful night's sleep, and all you hear is a chorus of "ribbits," and it's coming from your bed.

You can't take a shower without frogs ... you can't walk down the street without stepping on frogs ... you sit down to eat, and there are frogs hopping in and out of your food.

Frogs are in your stove and microwave oven ... you can't cook, you can't talk without frogs being at the center of your conversation.

The only thing as loud as the chorus of frogs singing is the noise of the people complaining about having to live with frogs everywhere.

When you ignore the voice of the Lord ... the warn-ings of the man of God ... then you will have to deal with the consequences of your actions or perhaps inaction as in the case of Pharaoh.

Exodus 8:8 says:

> *"Then Pharaoh called for Moses and Aaron, and said, Intreat the LORD, that he may take away the frogs from me, and from my people; and I will let the people go, that they may do sacrifice unto the LORD."*

Pharaoh promised to let the children of Israel go into the desert so they could offer a sacrifice to the Lord ... if only Moses would help get rid of Kermit and his friends.

Exodus 8:9 says:

> *"And Moses said unto Pharaoh, Glory over me: when shall I intreat for thee, and for thy servants, and for thy people, to destroy the frogs from thee and thy houses, that they may remain in the river only?"*

Moses repeats Pharaoh's promise and then states that he's going to ask God to have all the frogs jump back into the river. However, there is a very significant part of Exodus 8:10 we need to look at. It says:

> *"And he said, To morrow. And he said, Be it according to thy word: that thou mayest know that there is none like unto the LORD our God."*

Pharaoh agreed with Moses but said, "Tomorrow." Why would Pharaoh say "Tomorrow?"

If you've been up to your ankles in frogs ... why would you want to wait? If you knew that a particular course of action was the right thing to do for all concerned, why would you procrastinate?

Here are **four reasons why Pharaoh and others procrastinate.** Think about what ... if anything ... causes you to put things off.

First, you don't want to do what it is you say you will do.

If someone ... perhaps a spouse or otherwise asks you to do something that you really prefer not to do ... then you will find the most convenient excuse you can think of ... despite the fact that you agree to perform the task.

You may give one or more of the following reasons:

- I'm too tired.
- It's too late.
- I don't feel like it today.
- I'll do it tomorrow.
- Now is not a good time for me.
- It's too hot.
- It's too cold.
- Looks like it's going to rain.

I'm going to let you in on a little secret ... there have been times when I procrastinated in doing something simply because I really didn't want to do it. The really bad thing about this is that my fine wife, Bev, always knows when this is happening.

Has there ever been a time (or more than once) when you knew something needed to be done ... you said that you were going to do it ... but in your mind, you never seemed to find a convenient time ... or the motivation to do it?

It's obvious that Pharaoh wanted to get rid of the

frogs, but he also didn't want to let the children of Israel go.

Second, you don't feel like you're equipped to accomplish the task.

One of the main excuses given for procrastination is saying that you don't have everything you need to accomplish the specific task in front of you.

- I don't have the right tools.
- My computer doesn't have the necessary software.
- I don't have a truck.
- I don't have a car.

If God has called you to do something ... He will always make a way. God's calling is His enabling.

God will never allow you to see something without giving you the ability to accomplish it. That statement doesn't mean that work won't be involved. **You have to work to achieve everything in life.**

Hebrews 13:21 in the Amplified Bible says:

"Strengthen (complete, perfect) and make you what you ought to be and equip you with everything good that you may carry out His will; [while He Himself] works in you and accomplishes that which is pleasing in His sight, through Jesus Christ (the Messiah); to Whom be the glory

forever and ever (to the ages of the ages). Amen (so be it)."

Third, you don't feel the timing is right or convenient.

Have you ever thought, said or heard any of the following excuses?

- As soon as this television show is over, I'll do it.
- There's one more quarter left in the football game; I promise I'll get it done after the game.
- I planned to go fishing today.
- I have a golf date with the guys today; can't it wait?
- I'm having a girls' night out; I'll do it tomorrow.

Fourth, you assign other things a higher priority.

- I'll begin my new diet tomorrow.
- I'll write that report tomorrow.
- I'll start exercising tomorrow.

And the list could go on and on.

I'll make a statement, and I'll give you your response before you say or think it.

"If God asked you to do something, would you do it?"

And your answer would be "Absolutely," "Immediately" and of course "Without delay."

Yet God tells us to read, study, meditate and do His word. Are you doing it? If so, are you doing it on a consistent basis?

God tells us to spend time with Him in prayer. Are we doing it?

God tells us to care for the widows and the orphans ... are we doing it?

God tells us to tithe and give offerings ... are we doing it?

Psalm 119:60 in the New Living Translation says:

"I will hurry, without delay, to obey your commands."

One more thing, when we make a promise to God to do something ... we'd better do it and do it now. **He takes no pleasure in those who say "tomorrow," because He knows, and truthfully, so do you, that "tomorrow" never comes.**

Ecclesiastes 5:4 in the New Living Translation says:

"When you make a promise to God, don't delay in following through, for God takes no pleasure in fools. Keep all the promises you make to him."

Here's the bottom line ... if we delay or procrastinate, we might find ourselves still sleeping with the frogs.

Day 18

Turn Things Around

If you feel … you're headed in the wrong direction … or if it seems you're not making progress … today is the best day there'll ever be for you to turn things around.

Do you remember ever driving to a place you'd never been before … found yourself not knowing if you were heading in the right direction … but you still continued on?

I think this is particularly true … of most men … there is a hesitancy to stop and ask for directions … until it's clearly obvious that we're headed in the wrong direction.

There is an amazing parallel in life where some people know they're headed in the wrong direction, but they keep hesitating to make the decision to turn things around.

Jeremiah 8:4 in the Contemporary English Version says:

"[The People Took the Wrong Road] The LORD

said: People of Jerusalem, when you stumble and fall, you get back up, and if you take a wrong road, you turn around and go back."

The lifestyle turnaround begins with asking for forgiveness for our sins and returning to God.

Acts 3:19 in the Amplified Bible says:

"So repent (change your mind and purpose); turn around and return [to God], that your sins may be erased (blotted out, wiped clean), that times of refreshing (of recovering from the effects of heat, of reviving with fresh air) may come from the presence of the Lord."

If you think that's a great incentive for turning things around, then consider the words of Joel 2:13-14 in the Message Bible which say:

"Change your life, not just your clothes. Come back to God, your God. And here's why: God is kind and merciful. He takes a deep breath, puts up with a lot, This most patient God, extravagant in love, always ready to cancel catastrophe. Who knows? Maybe he'll do it now, maybe he'll turn around and show pity. Maybe, when all's said and done, there'll be blessings full and robust for your God!"

Sadly, there are some folks who think a new dress or a suit and a pair of shoes can turn things around.

Some people use an old saying that "Clothes make the man" to justify buying new clothes, but they either ignore or never knew the entire quote which came from Mark Twain, who actually said:

"Clothes make the man. Naked people have little or no influence on society."

As you can see, when taken in context, the quote is entirely different.

Way too many people spend money they don't have buying clothes in hopes that a new outward look will ease the inner pain they're experiencing … unfortunately that's not what happens.

An unwise shopping expedition only adds to your credit card balance, thus causing further problems.

The way to change your life is not with clothes, but through a renewed relationship with your Heavenly Father and a refreshed vision of why you were created in the first place

If one of your children has been acting foolishly or living a life of sin, but they convey honest repentance and a desire to come home seeking your forgiveness … you would, of course, welcome them with open arms.

You would be merciful, kind and generous with the love that you share with them.

That's the way our Heavenly Father is ... regardless of how sinful we've been ... He is ready and willing to receive us with open arms of love.

Not only that, but there will be "blessings full and robust from your God."

God will not only forgive your past sins ... He will forget them as well.

Ezekiel 18:21 in the Message Bible says:

> *"But a wicked person who turns his back on that life of sin and keeps all my statutes, living a just and righteous life, he'll live, really live. He won't die. **I won't keep a list of all the things he did wrong.** He will live. Do you think I take any pleasure in the death of wicked men and women? Isn't it my pleasure that they turn around, no longer living wrong but living right—really living?"*

Hallelujah!!! God will not keep a list of your past sins ... the things that you did wrong. Now that's something to shout about.

Not only that, but the scripture says that after you turn around to God ... you'll *"... live, really live."*

The only way to experience the abundant life that God desires for you is to turn around ... away from your sins ... turn your back on your past sinful habits and turn to Him.

Here's the exciting part ... **God takes pleasure in your turnaround.**

The exciting news is that He also takes pleasure in your prosperity.

Psalm 35:27 says:

> *"Let them shout for joy, and be glad, that favour my righteous cause: yea, let them say continually, Let the LORD be magnified, which hath pleasure in the prosperity of his servant."*

God's desire is for you to manifest the fullness of John 10:10 in the New Living Translation which says:

> *"The thief's purpose is to steal and kill and destroy. My purpose is to give them a rich and satisfying life."*

Your Heavenly Father is ready to receive you with open arms ... and to be actively involved in your decision to turn your life around. Just as a natural father wants the best for his children, so does your Heavenly Father wants the best for you.

Hear what I'm about to say ... please. Even if your natural father doesn't want the best for you, God does.

Psalm 27:10 in the Message Bible says:

> *"My father and mother walked out and left me,*

but God took me in."

Jeremiah 29:11-14 in the Message Bible says:

> *"I know what I'm doing. <u>I have it all planned out</u>—plans to take care of you, <u>not abandon you</u>, plans to give you the future you hope for. When you call on me, when you come and pray to me, I'll listen. When you come looking for me, you'll find me. 'Yes, when you get serious about finding me and want it more than anything else, I'll make sure you won't be disappointed.' God's Decree. '<u>I'll turn things around for you ... You can count on it</u>.' "*

Regardless of past mistakes ... when we seek Him ... receive His forgiveness ... then we "won't be disappointed."

When God tells you that you can count on something ... you can know it's going to happen. There are no "ifs," "ands" or "buts" ... it's going to happen.

God will *"... turn things around for you ... you can count on it."*

Not only does God want to bless you during your turnaround ... He wants you to represent the goodness of His Kingdom.

Isaiah 58:6 in the Message Bible says:

> *"This is the kind of fast day I'm after: to break*

the chains of injustice, get rid of exploitation in the workplace, free the oppressed, cancel debts. What I'm interested in seeing you do is: sharing your food with the hungry, inviting the homeless poor into your homes, putting clothes on the shivering ill-clad, being available to your own families. **Do this and the lights will turn on, and your lives will turn around at once.** *Your righteousness will pave your way. The God of glory will secure your passage. Then when you pray, God will answer. You'll call out for help and I'll say, 'Here I am.' "*

God wants you to be a force for righteousness … for financial deliverance … for humanitarian purposes … for providing for the needs of those less fortunate than you.

When you do what's right before Him … when you obey His instructions … when you call out for help … no matter what the problem … He'll say … *"Here I am."*

Now that's what I call a real turnaround in your life. Let it begin right now … with the next decision you make.

Day 19

A Mind Is a Terrible Thing To Waste

I have a unique dictionary in my library … it may not be politically correct, but it is spiritually accurate.

Years ago I cut the words "quit," "try," "compromise" and "can't" out of this dictionary. It was a symbolic gesture as I didn't want those words to be a part of my vocabulary … especially the word "can't."

The word "can't" when spoken by Christians in reference to God's will for their lives is grammatically or spiritually inaccurate. In fact, the word "can't" is contrary to the Word and will of God.

Philippians 4:13 says:

"I can do all things through Christ which strengtheneth me."

Personalize this verse with your name:

"[Name] can do all things through Christ which strengtheneth [her/him]."

There is no equivocation in this verse.

The key component of this passage is ... Christ's strength allows us to do all things.

Is getting out of debt a thing?

Is having a proper retirement income and investment portfolio a thing?

Is walking in divine health a thing?

Is having a peaceful and loving family life a thing?

Is being free of any and all addictions a thing?

Yes, and you can do all things through Christ which strengthens you.

Philippians 4:13 in the Amplified Bible says:

> *"I have strength for all things in Christ Who empowers me [I am ready for anything and equal to anything through Him Who infuses inner strength into me; I am self-sufficient in Christ's sufficiency]."*

God wants us to be self-sufficient in Him.

Are we self-sufficient when we're depending on the government, family and friends; or some agency to put food on our table?

Of course not. Make no mistake about it. God wants you to be self-sufficient.

Your natural (logical) mind will tell you that what I've just put before you from the Word of God is not possible. That thought … is the limitation of a natural mind. Or you might think it applies to everybody else but you … that is a lie straight from the pit of hell.

Don't let the enemy steal self-sufficiency from you.

You must believe, embrace and exercise what the scripture says in 1 Corinthians 2:16 in the Amplified Bible:

> *"For who has known or understood the mind (the counsels and purposes) of the Lord so as to guide and instruct Him and give Him knowledge? But we have the mind of Christ (the Messiah) and do **hold the thoughts (feelings and purposes) of His heart."***

You and I have the mind of Christ. Not only that but we have the same feelings, thoughts and purposes that He does.

We must believe what the scripture says … if we have the mind of Christ then we **can bring every thought captive to the obedience of God.**

2 Corinthians 10:5 says:

> *"Casting down imaginations, and every high*

thing that exalteth itself against the knowledge of God, and bringing into captivity every thought to the obedience of Christ."

You see, at this point, we have a choice.

We can either believe the natural mind (things that we've heard over the years, things that we've been taught by people through natural logic and reasoning, the information we've gathered from people who don't accept Jesus as the Lord of their lives; or in other words who are not living out the Word) or we can simply believe what the Word of God says is true.

With the mind of Christ ... I can fully accept, appreciate and activate the principles of His Word when it says that "I can do all things through Christ which strengthens me," and so can you.

Here is how this process works.

Your natural mind is saying, "No, you can't do that. You don't have the education for it. You've never done anything like that before. No, you can't."

Your spiritual mind is saying, "Yes, you can! Yes, you can! The Word says you can do all things through Christ."

If you say "I can't," then you are giving place, strength, power and authority to what you perceive to be your inabilities to achieve <u>what God Himself said you can do</u>.

However, **if you say "I can do all things," you are intensifying, fortifying and magnifying that ability in your life.** You are choosing the spirit over the natural.

Now, I fully realize that saying "I can" doesn't make a thing happen immediately. It does, however, bring it one step closer to making it happen.

By speaking the Word of God, you are enabling or "feeding" God's thoughts; and by refusing to speak negative disabling thoughts, you strengthen the possibility, probability and inevitability of the thing that you're speaking coming to pass.

It is imperative that you begin to speak what the mind of Christ within you is saying is possible.

When you speak the words that are from the mind of Christ, it unleashes a spiritual dynamic in the earth. Besides, you are not the one who is making it happen by your strength. God's Word is coming through your mouth.

Joel 3:10 says:

> *"Beat your plowshares into swords and your pruninghooks into spears: <u>let the weak say, I am strong</u>."*

The Amplified Translation of Joel 3:10 says:

> *"Beat your plowshares into swords, and your*

pruning hooks into spears; let the weak say, I am strong [a warrior]!"

You need to begin to speak that strength ... it makes you battle ready.

Now consider the words of Joel 3:9-11 in the Message Bible:

"Announce this to the godless nations: Prepare for battle! Soldiers at attention! Present arms! Advance! Turn your shovels into swords, turn your hoes into spears. Let the weak one throw out his chest and say, 'I'm tough, I'm a fighter.' Hurry up, pagans! Wherever you are, get a move on! Get your act together. Prepare to be shattered by God!"

Not only are you preparing to destroy every enemy of your success ... you see things through the mind of Christ.

Romans 4:17 in the Amplified Bible says:

"As it is written, I have made you the father of many nations. [He was appointed our father] in the sight of God in Whom he believed, Who gives life to the dead and speaks of the nonex-istent things that [He has foretold and promised] as if they [already] existed."

The Message Bible translates Romans 4:17-18 like

this:

> *"We call Abraham 'father' not because he got God's attention by living like a saint, but because* **God made something out of Abraham when he was a nobody.** *Isn't that what we've always read in Scripture, God saying to Abraham, 'I set you up as father of many peoples?' Abraham was first named 'father' and then became a father because* **he dared to trust God to do what only God could do:** *raise the dead to life,* **with a word make something out of nothing.** *When everything was hopeless, Abraham believed anyway,* **deciding to live not on the basis of what he saw he couldn't do but on what God said he would do** *..."*

Child of God, get hold of this ... God made something of Abraham when he was nothing ... a nobody. You may feel like you're a nothing, BUT GOD can and will make something out of you. But like Abraham, you must decide not to live on the basis of what you see and think you "can't" do ... but rather on the basis of what God's Word says <u>you can do</u>.

For years, the United Negro College Fund has had an incredible slogan which says "A mind is a terrible thing to waste." That's especially true ... when it's the mind of Christ that's in you saying that you can do all things through Him!

Isn't it time you begin to think like Him?

God Is Going To Pay You

Day 20

In sales training years ago, I learned and subsequently taught what is referred to as *deflect*, *defer* and *redirect*.

If you're making your sales pitch, and the potential customer or client were to ask a question that interrupts your presentation ... that's where you use the technique of deflect, defer and redirect. Here's an example.

"That's a good question." *Deflect*.

"I'll get back to your question in a moment." *Defer*.

"Have you ever considered the benefits of owning this widget or gizmo?" *Redirect*.

Truthfully, I suggest you employ the <u>deflect, defer and redirect</u> strategy on attacks of the enemy.

"Devil, I'm wise to your tricks, traps, lies and deceit." ***Deflect.***

"That's not going to work on me today, because the

Word of God says ..." *Defer.*

"I'm praying for God to give me an opportunity today ... to be a blessing to someone else. I'm also praying for the salvation of ..." *Redirect.*

When you're in the midst of a crisis, it's imperative for you to get your eyes off your problem ... stop talking about it ... stop rehearsing your hurts and pains.

Instead, put your focus on doing good for someone else ... it works because it's a totally biblical principle, and as an added benefit ... it drives the devil crazier. (He's already crazy!)

I feel Ephesians 6:8 is one of the most powerful verses in the Bible. It's the scripture that describes the essence of who I am in Him. The Amplified Bible translation says:

> *"Knowing that for whatever good anyone does, he will receive his reward from the Lord, whether he is slave or free."*

Give of yourself ... your time ... and see what you get in return. It will amaze you.

When you give something of great value ... it moves God.

Day after day I read letters from people who tell me they have nothing to give. They even confess how broke they are ... which is the worst possible thing they could do.

If you say you have nothing to give, then you're ignoring your greatest treasure on planet earth ... your time.

I've discovered that many of the people who say they have nothing to give are overlooking the valuable asset of their time.

If you're unemployed ... or between jobs ... what are you doing with your time?

Let me give you a revelation ... if you have a need in your life ... **then turn your need into seed.**

Do you need more time to accomplish your job or your goals? Would you like to have more time with your family? **Then sow time into the lives of others.**

Hebrews 13:16 in the Amplified Bible says:

> "*Do not forget or neglect to do kindness and good, to be generous and distribute and contribute to the needy [of the church as embodiment and proof of fellowship], for <u>such sacrifices are pleasing to God</u>.*"

Do you want to do something that is pleasing to God? Then do something that costs you something important ... your time.

The Message Bible translation of Hebrews 13:16 says:

> *"Make sure you don't take things for granted and go slack in working for the common good; share what you have with others. God takes particular pleasure in acts of worship—a different kind of "sacrifice"—that take place in kitchen and workplace and on the streets."*

The scripture says "… share what you have with others."

What do you have? Time.

Here are 13 ways in which you can sow your time into the lives of others.

1. Visit the homes of widows in your church … clean up around their houses.

2. Clean a neighborhood park or place where children play.

3. Ask your pastor if you can volunteer to help out around the church.

You may be needed to vacuum the sanctuary … wax the floors … cut the grass or even clean the toilets.

The first job that Willie George ever had in the church after getting saved was cleaning toilets. He became a servant first, and then he became Gospel Bill on

Christian TV and Pastor of Church on the Move in Tulsa, Oklahoma.

The question isn't how you view doing menial jobs as an act of service, but rather **how God views your attitude about being a blessing to others through your time.**

One more thing, if your efforts around the church frees your pastor to study the Word or increase his effectiveness in other areas … just think what God is going to do for you.

4. Drive widows or shut-ins to various medical or other appointments.

5. Do the grocery shopping for those who can't get out.

6. Mow the grass and maintain the landscaping for senior citizens. Rake their leaves in the fall or shovel snow as needed in the winter.

7. Change the oil in the vehicles of widows and/or single mothers.

8. Prepare food and/or baked goods for elderly people or those who are shut-in.

9. Visit the sick, the elderly and the lonely … in their homes, hospitals or nursing homes.

10. Provide child care for a single mother while she

goes grocery shopping or just has a little alone time. (Make sure to set boundaries on your time ... do not allow your kindness to be taken advantage of.)

11. Write a thank you note to your local fire and/or police department ... thanking them for their services. On special holidays ... bake some cookies and/or a cake to share with these emergency service personnel.

12. Collect household items, toys and other goodies for widows, orphans and those who are enduring temporary financial setbacks. Fix broken toys for children. Gather coats in the fall for distribution to those in need.

13. Rake a neighbor's leaves or offer to help with other major projects.

The list could go on and on, but hopefully you're getting the idea. **Reach beyond yourself to help others** ... _by investing your time to bless them_.

Matthew 12:35 in the Message Bible says:

"It's your heart, not the dictionary that gives meaning to your words. A good person produces good deeds and words season after season ..."

Galatians 6:10 in the Amplified Bible says:

"So then, as occasion and opportunity open up to us, let us do good [morally] to all people [not *only being useful or profitable to them, but also doing what is for their spiritual good and advantage]. Be mindful to be a blessing, especially to those of the household of faith [those who belong to God's family with you, the believers]."*

Where do you start? Well, this scripture gives you a clear indication of what you should be doing first. Begin investing your time in those who "… belong to God's family with you."

One more thing, there is a spiritual dynamic that takes place when you begin helping the widows, orphans and the poor.

Proverbs 19:17 in the New Living Translation says:

"If you help the poor, you are lending to the Lord—and he will repay you!"

When you help the widows, the orphans, poor and elderly … you are actually positioning yourself for a reward … a harvest of blessings.

When you cut someone's grass, you're saving them inconvenience and money.

When you change someone's oil … you're saving them inconvenience and money.

When you run errands for others, you're saving them inconvenience and money.

When you save someone else money ... that's funds they can redirect somewhere else. By sowing your time to make others more effective stewards of their resources ... you've got to know ... God is going to do that same thing for you.

The activation of Ephesians 6:8 in your life ... will change you inside, and yes, even your financial destiny.

> *"Knowing that for whatever good anyone does, he will receive his reward from the Lord, whether he is slave or free."*

Get ready ... **the Lord is about to repay you** ... for what **you've done for others.**

Day 21

Who Is God Unwilling To Do Without?

I never cease to be amazed at how some people can take one verse of scripture and twist it to suit their purposes and/or lifestyle.

For instance, 2 Corinthians 9:7 says:

> *"Every man according as he purposeth in his heart, <u>so let him give</u>; not grudgingly, or of necessity: for God loveth a cheerful giver."*

Believe it or not, this verse is often cited by some Christians as a justification for not tithing.

They say the scripture tells them to be cheerful givers, and that they cannot give up 10% of their income cheerfully. They would feel better about 3% or maybe even 5% ... but 10% is way too much. They say tithing is Old Testament legalism.

This type of thinking ... or lack thereof ... is wrong on several different levels.

First, if you think tithing is part of the old covenant ... I encourage you to visit www.haroldherring.com and search for my teaching, "A Fresh Look at New Testament Tithing."

Second, such comments are scripturally dangerous. It would lead others to think and act based on feelings and emotions, and not the whole Word of God.

There is a hedonistic philosophy that suggests, "If it feels good, do it," or even worse, "If it feels good, do it again."

What if we applied this same logic ... to other basic Christian principles?

We only pray if we are in the mood or are facing a real emergency.

We only attend church when it is convenient and doesn't interfere with other things we feel like doing.

We do good to others as long as we feel they are doing good to us ... and only if they do it first and we feel good about it.

We honor our mother and father only if they give us what we want.

We only worship God if we really like the music and feel like singing and lifting our hands in praise.

If a person subscribes to the philosophy of only

doing what they can do cheerfully ... then many people would probably never go to work ... or fix things around the house ... or help others in need.

They would backslide in their faith and fall away from the things of God.

Please understand that I'm not saying you can't do all these things cheerfully ... but <u>the Bible teaches us not to be controlled by or respond to the leading of our emotions</u>. And even if we were led that way, some people aren't cheerful about anything, anyway.

<u>Any attempt to justify not tithing and giving offerings because it wouldn't make you happy is a weak, lame alibi;</u> and excuses about why we can't obey Him don't impress God.

Interestingly enough, the dictionary defines *alibi* as:

"an excuse to avoid blame."

Now let me ask you several questions:

Has there <u>ever been a time when you didn't tithe or stopped tithing for a short period of time</u>?

If a person, a robber, <u>takes what doesn't belong to him even once in a while</u>, does that **make him any less of a thief**?

If the **robber only steals when he/she wants or**

needs money, does that make them any less of a thief?

If you've ever watched a television program or movie about criminals, you know **the first thing the defense attorney wants to know is if they have an alibi.**

The attorney will advise his/her client whether or not they have a "good" alibi, the kind that will stand up in court and get them off the hook.

Do you have an alibi for not tithing or giving offerings to God's work?

Will it stand up in the Court of Heaven? **Will God accept it on Judgment Day**?

Is the Word of God based on your view of your circumstances, or what the Word says about the subject?

For those who really want to be cheerful on Judgment Day ... I suggest they forget the alibis and obey the Word of God.

2 Corinthians 9:7 concludes by saying "... *for God loveth a cheerful giver.*"

According to Strong's Concordance, *cheerful* is the Greek word *hilaros* which only appears in the New Testament one time and means:

"cheerful, joyous, prompt to do anything."

The English word *hilarious* comes from this word, and the implication is that we are to be very joyful givers. Now let's look at 2 Corinthians 9:7 in the Amplified Bible which says:

> *"Let each one [give] as he has made up his own mind and purposed in his heart, not reluctantly or sorrowfully or under compulsion, for God loves (He takes pleasure in, prizes above other things, and is unwilling to abandon or to do without) a cheerful (joyous, 'prompt to do it') giver [whose heart is in his giving]."*

God created you to be an agent of free will … meaning you have a choice to obey or not obey. The spiritual benefits of tithing and giving cheerfully should make you smile … BIG TIME.

Every believer should become hilariously happy when they realize the incredible benefits that paying tithes and giving offerings bring.

Giving can be a happy, joyous experience even when you are poor. You might be saying … really?

Consider what 2 Corinthians 8:1-4 in the New Living Translation says:

> *"Now I want you to know, dear brothers and sisters, what God in his kindness has done through the churches in Macedonia. They are being tested by many troubles, and they are very poor.*

But they are also filled with abundant joy, which has overflowed in rich generosity.

"For I can testify that they gave not only what they could afford, but far more. And they did it of their own free will. They begged us again and again for the privilege of sharing in the gift for the believers in Jerusalem."

The churches in Macedonia understood that the time to give is when things are tough ... because that's the only way out of the situation.

It's clear in 2 Corinthians 9:7 that the Apostle Paul was seeking to motivate fellow believers to give out of a true "love for God" motive. <u>He was pointing out the benefits of proper giving</u>. He definitely wasn't creating a loophole for those looking for an excuse not to give; but rather an incentive to do it properly.

I had a former pastor who used to say that God loves a cheerful giver, but He will take it from a grouch. There was a time I liked that, because it was a funny statement, until I realized that it is, in fact, scripturally inaccurate.

The scripture says that God loves a cheerful, hilarious, joyous, prompt to do it giver. **So, if you're not happy in your giving ... then you've got to know that God isn't into your giving, either.**

In other words, if *"... He takes pleasure in, prizes above other things, and is unwilling to abandon or to do without) a cheerful (joyous, 'prompt to do it') giver [whose heart is in his giving]"* ... then anything else doesn't make Him happy.

Make no mistake about it ... the local church, the ministry or non-profit organizations may take your money and be happy about it ... but that doesn't make your money pleasing to God.

Truthfully, **I'm much more interested and motivated about how God looks on my giving than I am about my personal feelings,** because my flesh will always offer a ready excuse.

- Do you want God to take pleasure in you?

- Do you want God to prize you about all things?

- Do you want God to never abandon you?

Then your answer is clear ... be a cheerful, even hilarious giver ... prompt to give what He says to give ... regardless of your circumstances.

When God directs you to give and you obey His instructions ... it draws you closer to Him on a number of levels. Bottom line ... your money shows God that your heart is towards Him.

Day 22

6 Differences Between Successful and Unsuccessful People

Have you ever read a scripture that just ignited a mental firestorm …
stirring your spirit and energizing your fingers on a laptop keyboard?

Here's the scripture that fired me up today.

Proverbs 12:24 in the New Living Translation says:

"Work hard and become a leader; be lazy and become a slave."

As I read that scripture I began thinking about the differences between successful and unsuccessful people.

Brian Tracy, the noted author and success teacher, said:

"Successful people are always looking for opportunities to help others. Unsuccessful people are always asking, 'What's in it for me?' "

<u>Being successful is not necessarily the result of your education, experience, family background or luck</u> ... <u>but neither is being unsuccessful the result of those same things</u>.

Here are six differences between successful and unsuccessful people.

1. Successful people make plans ... unsuccessful people make excuses.

2 Thessalonians 3:10 in the Message Bible says:

"Don't you remember the rule we had when we lived with you? 'If you don't work, you don't eat.' And now we're getting reports that a bunch of lazy good-for-nothings are taking advantage of you. This must not be tolerated. We command them to get to work immediately—no excuses, no arguments—and earn their own keep. Friends, don't slack off in doing your duty."

If you spend your life looking for an excuse ... you'll never find the time to discover the solution to your problems.

If you're good at making excuses ... you'll never be good at anything else.

Proverbs 21:5 in the New International Version says:

"The plans of the diligent lead to profit as surely

as haste leads to poverty."

I've written extensively on both *plans* and *excuses* in the past. Visit our website www.haroldherring.com and do a search for both topics.

<u>People with excuses will never be remembered for what they did ... or even what they could have done</u>.

2. Successful people live disciplined lives ... unsuccessful people do what feels good at the moment.

Leading a disciplined financial life is saying *no* to impulse buying ... and *yes* to becoming debt free.

A disciplined financial life is saying *no* today so you can have a better tomorrow.

If you remember, Proverbs 12:24 says that ... if we don't work hard ... we won't be a leader but will, in fact, become a slave.

Proverbs 22:7 in the Contemporary English Version says:

> *"The poor are ruled by the rich, and those who borrow are slaves of moneylenders."*

Financial discipline today will keep you from being a slave to someone else tomorrow.

Let me say it another way: If you lead an undisciplined

financial life, instead of spending your retirement years visiting your grandchildren, family and friends ... you'll be greeting your family and friends as they walk through the doors of McDonalds or Wal-Mart.

Make the tough decisions now ... so you don't have to live a life without choices later.

3. **Successful people associate with those who have dreams and goals ... unsuccessful people associate with wishers. They wish they had a better life but never do anything about it.**

You are blessed or cursed by the people you associate with. Let me say that same sentence but in a different manner.

You will either be successful or unsuccessful by the people you associate with.

Make a list of your seven closest friends and associates.

Now ask yourself these four questions ... which I've asked before in my teachings ... but they bear repeating.

What does this person add to my life?

What's the greatest negative influence this person has on my life?

What's the last positive idea, scripture or thought this person shared with me?

Does this person motivate me to be all I can be in Him?

It only makes sense to associate with people who can encourage, exhort, edify and build you up as you pursue your dreams of success. <u>Surround yourself with people who also have a dream, a goal and a vision of what they want their lives to be</u>.

1 Corinthians 15:33 in the Amplified Bible says:

> *"Do not be so deceived and misled! Evil companionships (communion, associations) corrupt and deprave good manners and morals and character."*

4. Successful people are never thrown by obstacles to their success … unsuccessful people whine about how unfair things are.

What or who's the greatest obstacle or limitation you face in achieving your goals? LOOK IN A MIRROR for your answer … because it's you.

When you look in that mirror, you need to be looking with the eye of the Spirit.

Don't look with the natural eye at your physical appearance or what you're wearing. Forget what people have said, or even more importantly, what you have thought about your own abilities and failures in the past.

When you look in that mirror, you need to realize that you're not alone. You've got the Father, Son and Holy Spirit working on your team.

Deuteronomy 28:8 in the Contemporary English Version says:

> "The LORD your God is giving you the land, and he will make sure you are successful in everything you do. Your harvests will be so large that your storehouses will be full."

Personalize this with your name:

> "The LORD [Name]'s God is giving [him/her] the land, and he will make sure [Name] is successful in everything [he/she] does. [Name]'s harvests will be so large that [his/her] storehouses will be full."

I could give you a number of reasons why whining is a bad idea ... but all I need to give you is one. God doesn't like it.

Numbers 11:10 in the Message Bible says:

> "Moses heard the whining, all those families whining in front of their tents. God's anger blazed up. Moses saw that things were in a bad way."

5. Successful people manage their time and their lives ... unsuccessful people wonder what happened to their time.

You decide ... not somebody else ... not the passing of time on a clock ... you decide what you will do with every minute of every day God has given to you. Don't be discouraged by others. There is a way around every hindrance.

Nehemiah 6:9 in the New Living Translation says:

"They were just trying to intimidate us, imagining that they could discourage us and stop the work. So I continued the work with even greater determination."

God wants us to take charge of our divine destiny with a firm determination to make our days count.

Psalm 90:12 in the Contemporary English Version says:

"Teach us to use wisely all the time we have."

Here's a revelation ... the title of the Rolling Stones song, *Time Is On My Side*, can be a reality in your life ... if you make the right choices.

Your Heavenly Father wants you to maximize your time ... using every second of every day for His greater glory. It's time to be about His business.

6. Successful people are willing to make tough decisions ... unsuccessful people always look for the easy way out.

If you were to ask the average person if they were a coward...they would rather emphatically respond with a vigorous "NO." However, that response is likely being offered in good times; the real question of character and intestinal fortitude is determined when times are tough.

Jeremiah 46:20 in the Message Bible says:

> *"Too bad, Egypt, a beautiful sleek heifer attacked by a horsefly from the north! All her hired soldiers are stationed to defend her— like well-fed calves they are. But when their lives are on the line, they'll run off, cowards everyone. When the going gets tough, they'll take the easy way out."*

What appears to be the easy way out of adverse circumstances most often turns into a slippery slope of failure and disillusionment.

If you want to become successful, debt free and have more than enough ... there will be times when you have to make tough decisions. You may have to say "no" to your children or to something you had wanted to buy for yourself.

God highly respects those who can make tough

decisions … who will stand and fight for what's right on the journey to a better way of life.

Day 23

6 More Differences Between Successful and Unsuccessful People

On Day 22, I shared six differences between successful and unsuccessful people. Before continuing this teaching, I want to share this quote by Brian Tracy one more time. He said:

"Successful people are always looking for opportunities to help others. Unsuccessful people are always asking, 'What's in it for me?' "

Here are six more differences between successful and unsuccessful people.

1. **Successful people realize success is a journey, not a destination ... unsuccessful people don't have a clue where they're going nor how to get there.**

Arthur Ashe, one of the renowned tennis greats, said:

"Success is a journey not a destination. The doing is usually more important than the outcome. Not

everyone can be Number 1."

When you focus on success as a journey instead of a destination ... you have the potential to experience some sort of success ... every day. You don't have to wait until you arrive to experience the exhilaration and satisfaction of success.

<u>Your ultimate and lasting success is based on what you learn, overcome and endure on your trip from where you are to where God wants you to be</u> ... and make no mistake about it, He wants you to be successful.

As you begin your journey ... the first thing you should do is to seek Godly wisdom in every decision you make.

Judges 18:5 in the New Living Translation says:

"Then they said, 'Ask God whether or not our journey will be successful.' "

2. **Successful people are focused on their future ... unsuccessful people are focused on what they're doing today and this weekend.**

The enemy's number one tactic in delaying and/or destroying your future success is to break your focus ... or cause you to focus on things that are inconsequential to your future success.

Sadly, some people's idea of long-range planning is

whether to eat at Denny's, IHOP or Cracker Barrel this weekend.

Luke 9:41 in the Message Bible says:

> *"Jesus said, 'What a generation! No sense of God! No focus to your lives! How many times do I have to go over these things? How much longer do I have to put up with this?' "*

I think it's fairly obvious that God wants us focused on our future success and not just stuff.

Philippians 3:15-16 in the Message Bible says:

> *"So let's keep focused on that goal, those of us who want everything God has for us. If any of you have something else in mind, something less than total commitment, God will clear your blurred vision—you'll see it yet! Now that we're on the right track, let's stay on it."*

Focus can be simply defined as "whatever has your attention." If focus is important to God, then it should be important to us.

3. Successful people are closers and finishers ... unsuccessful people rarely complete a goal or a project.

Have you ever started an assignment or job with a sudden burst of enthusiasm only to be slowed down by the first obstacle, and you were stopped short of your goal by continual obstacles?

Congratulations, you're normal ... average ... but you don't have to stay that way.

The strength of a person's character and drive to success is determined by whether or not they can finish what they started.

Employees who complete the task are more highly valued than those who, though they make a valiant effort, nevertheless fail to complete the project.

The One by whom our every effort, thought and action should be measured ... was a finisher.

John 4:34 in the New Living Translation says:

> *"Then Jesus explained: 'My nourishment comes from doing the will of God, who sent me, and from finishing his work.' "*

Not only was Jesus a finisher, but he made us that way as well.

Philippians 1:6 in the New Living Translation says:

> *"And I am certain that God, who began the good work within you, will continue his work until it is finally finished on the day when Christ Jesus returns."*

Personalize this … Vitali … Irene … Vincent …

> *"And I am certain that God, who began the good work within [Name], will continue his work until it is finally finished on the day when Christ Jesus returns."*

4. Successful people understand that success is about more than money … unsuccessful people think success is only what they see on television.

If you were to ask most people what success means to them … they would cite the acquisition of expensive and exquisite things, the kind of things you'd see on the "Lifestyles of the Rich and Famous." The kind of things that make others go "oooh, ahhh" such as: an expensive new house, a new luxury car, designer clothes, valuable jewelry and the kind of vacations that only a few enjoy but millions of others dream about.

But what does the Bible say about success? Joshua 1:8 says:

> *"This book of the law shall not depart out of thy mouth; but thou shalt meditate therein day and night, that thou mayest observe to do according to all that is written therein: for then thou shalt make thy way prosperous, and then thou shalt have good success."*

There are two things we should notice in this passage.

First, we're responsible for our own prosperity and success. The word *thou* and *thy* are mentioned six times in this verse. In contemporary translations, the words are *you* and *your*. Regardless of the translation, the message is the same ... **whether or not you're successful and prosperous is a result of the decisions you make and the actions you take.**

Second, the word *success* is the Hebrew word *sakal* (H7919) and it means:

> **"to be prudent, to have insight, give attention to, wisely understand, act wisely and prosper."**

Success is not what you have but rather who you become.

5. **Successful people are willing to overlook jealousy and prejudice ... unsuccessful people let other people stand in the way of pursuing their dreams.**

Jealously causes people to do some crazy things.

Most people want you to succeed in life ... as long as you're not more successful than they are.

Too many believers have allowed others to plant things in their subconscious response mechanism that makes them jealous, critical and prejudiced against people who have succeeded where they have failed.

God does not take kindly to those who do. Proverbs 17:5 in the New Living Translation says:

"Those who mock the poor insult their Maker; those who rejoice at the misfortune of others will be punished."

> **A successful person is always blessed and motivated by the successful testimony of others, knowing it won't be long before they'll be joining them.**

Romans 12:15 in the Amplified Bible says:

"Rejoice with those who rejoice [sharing others' joy], and weep with those who weep [sharing others' grief]."

When we get as excited about somebody else's success as we are our own ... we can watch out, because success is about to overtake us.

6. Successful people pay attention to details ... unsuccessful people are bored by the ordinary.

Someone once said, "Take care of the little things,

and the big things will take care of themselves."

If you've ever wondered how God feels about attention to details being fundamental to your success ... I suggest you listen to 2 Corinthians 6:2-3 in the Message Bible very carefully. It says:

> *"Well, now is the right time to listen, the day to be helped. Don't put it off; don't frustrate God's work by showing up late, throwing a question mark over everything we're doing. Our work as God's servants gets validated—or not—in the details ..."*

The difference between ordinary and extraordinary is found in the attention that's given to the details.

If the devil can break your focus on what's necessary for success ... then he has disrupted and delayed, if not destroyed your destiny.

There is actually one other main difference between unsuccessful and successful people ... and that's YOU.

You're the one who will determine whether or not your life is successful. It's you. Nobody else but you.

Day
24

God Can Use Anything Anybody Anytime

God can use anything, anybody, at any time to meet your needs in the midst of a financial drought.

Regardless of what you're going through ... take comfort ... your answer is on the way.

Write that down ... my answer is on the way. No matter what you're facing ... YOUR ANSWER IS ON THE WAY.

1 Kings 17:2-4 says:

> *"And the word of the LORD came unto him, saying, Get thee hence, and turn thee eastward, and hide thyself by the brook Cherith that is before Jordan. And it shall be, that thou shalt drink of the brook; and I have commanded the ravens to feed thee there."*

Elijah had just delivered a Word from the Lord by telling the king and the people about a drought and famine that were to come. Then God sent Elijah to a brook called Cherith where he told him to drink of the brook and that he would be fed by ravens.

Now to the natural mind you have to consider how strange it was for anyone to be fed by ravens ... as they are nasty, selfish scavengers who pick the flesh off dead animals.

When I get to heaven one of the questions I want to ask Elijah is what he first thought when the Lord informed him that he would be fed by ravens.

Did he think, "You're kidding me; they're nasty birds and probably carry disease. God, how about eagles? They're majestic, and if not them, how about at least some carrier pigeons?"

Elijah didn't know and probably didn't care where the ravens got the food. They were no doubt directed someplace where people were baking fresh bread or roasting delicious meat.

> The bottom line is this ... **God provided for Elijah in the midst of the famine** even if it was not in a way that he might have expected.

When circumstances changed and the brook dried up, the ravens stopped coming with food ... in 1 Kings 17:8, the scripture says that a word came to Elijah telling him what to do next. Elijah was sent to the widow at Zarephath.

1 Kings 17:9 says:

> *"Arise, get thee to Zarephath, which belongeth to Zidon, and dwell there: behold, I have commanded a widow woman there to sustain thee."*

Again, in the natural, Elijah may have thought that finally God was sending him to be provided for by a wealthy widow woman. He probably imagined she had a fine house … maybe a servant or two and certainly plenty of food.

If you're familiar with the story of the widow at Zarephath, you know that none of that was true.

In 1 Kings 17:10-11, Elijah tells the widow what to do.

> *"So he arose and went to Zarephath. And when he came to the gate of the city, behold, the widow woman was there gathering of sticks: and he called to her, and said, Fetch me, I pray thee, a little water in a vessel, that I may drink. And as she was going to fetch it, he called to her, and said, Bring me, I pray thee, a morsel of bread in thine hand."*

The widow told the Man of God that she was broke, down to her last meal, which she planned to share with her son, then prepare to die.

1 Kings 17:12 says:

> *"And she said, As the LORD thy God liveth, I have not a cake, but an handful of meal in a barrel, and a little oil in a cruse: and, behold, I am gathering two sticks, that I may go in and dress it for me and my son, that we may eat it, and die."*

Elijah didn't say, "I'm so sorry. Had I known your situation, I never would have asked for your food. God must have somebody else that can provide for me."

On the contrary, at this point the prophet realized that this widow woman was about to receive miracle manifestation. Once again, God was providing for him in a totally unexpected manner.

1 Kings 17:13-16 in the New Living Translation says:

> *"But Elijah said to her, **'Don't be afraid!** <u>Go ahead</u> and **do just what you've said**, but make a little bread for me first. Then use what's left to prepare a meal for yourself and your son. For this is what the Lord, the God of Israel, says: There will always be flour and olive oil left in your containers until the time when the Lord sends rain and the crops grow again!' So she did as Elijah said, and she and Elijah and her son continued to eat for many days. There was always enough flour and olive oil left in the containers, just as the Lord had promised through Elijah."*

Notice the very first thing Elijah said: "Don't be afraid." God always has an answer even if it seems altogether unusual.

It's important to realize that **the manner in which God gets provision to you can change instantly, and it can seem unusual** … that's why it's important to stay plugged in to the Word of the Lord … listening for His direction for your next steps.

Psalm 32:8 in the Amplified Bible says:

> *"I [the Lord] will instruct you and teach you in the way you should go; I will counsel you with My eye upon you."*

It's important to know that God will instruct **YOU** and teach **YOU** in the way **YOU** should go. He will counsel **YOU** with His eye upon **YOU**. Take comfort in those words.

In fact, this is one scripture that I'm continually urging people to personalize.

This is for you … Kimberly … Paul … Janine …

> *"I [the Lord] will instruct [your name] and teach [your name] in the way [he/she] should go; I will counsel [your name] with My eye upon [him, her, them]."*

Make this scripture a part of your daily confession.

Psalm 32:8 is the key to God's plan for the provision and direction of our lives. He will instruct and teach us ... but we must take steps of faith.

Don't look to your friends or those who are generous and financially successful to meet your needs ... look to the Lord. He is your only source. He will direct you to the path that you're to follow.

Psalm 37:23 in the Amplified Bible says:

> *"The steps of a [good] man are directed and established by the Lord when He delights in his way [and He busies Himself with his every step]."*

The New Living Translation says that He will delight *"... in every detail of their lives."*

God will make certain that your every step is secure ... even when you're not sure what's happening.

The key is looking to Him ... not somebody else ... but Him ...

God can use anything, anybody, at any time to meet your needs ...

He may choose to use a scavenger bird like the raven to provide for you ...

He may choose a destitute widow woman to provide for you ...

He may choose to use your current employer to provide for you …

He may choose to use an inheritance to provide for you …

He may choose someone you know or someone you've never met to provide for you … but the bottom line is … God will provide for you.

Don't doubt … don't despair … hold fast to the confession of your faith … help is on the way.

Be expectant … anticipate the manifestation … know that God is not a man that He should lie. What He's said … He will bring to pass.

Deuteronomy 31:6 in the Message Bible says:

> *"God, your God, is striding ahead of you. He's right there with you. He won't let you down; he won't leave you. Don't be intimidated. Don't worry."*

God Could Bring Anything, Anybody, at Any Time to Anyplace to Meet Your Needs … and Yes, on This Day … YOUR ANSWER IS ON THE WAY.

7 Surprises God Has For You

Day 25

Some years ago while waiting for an airplane flight, I had the pleasure of meeting Jim Nabors. He is known to millions as Gomer Pyle whose character was made famous on the Andy Griffith television show. And by the way, he sounds totally different in real life.

Gomer, who also had a television show named after him for a short time, was famous for saying, "Surprise. Surprise. Surprise." That seems to be what's happening around us on a daily basis.

Here's a revelation for you ... **despite the changing political and financial landscape, God is not surprised by what's happening on planet earth, and that includes every detail of your life**.

Our Heavenly Father may be disappointed by some of the things He sees going on ... but he is not surprised or caught off guard in the least.

The majority of people are hurting ... fearful ... unsure

... and that includes believers who attend church every time the door is open. An atmosphere of doubt seems to be very pervasive right now.

If you're expecting the dawn of each new day to bring more unsettling news, then you won't be disappointed ... like Job, the thing you dread will come upon you.

Job 3:25 says:

> "For the thing which I greatly feared is come upon me, and that which I was afraid of is come unto me."

It's important to realize that expectation can be positive or negative.

You can expect the immediate manifestation for seed that you've sown ... that's positive.

However, you can also doubt that you'll ever receive a harvest for what you've sown ... that's negative expectation, and you'd also be right.

You can expect the promotion that you've worked hard to achieve ... that's positive.

However, if you believe someone else always gets your promotions even though you deserve them ... that's negative expectation, and again, you'd be right.

You can expect God's healing virtue to flow over you

… that's positive.

However, if you doubt that divine healing is for today … that's a negative expectation, and you'd be right.

Whatever you expect … is exactly what you'll manifest in your life … positive or negative … good or bad. Expect His best … and you won't be disappointed.

If you expect bad news … if you live with a Worst Case Scenario mentality … that's exactly what you're going to get.

Malcolm Forbes, the founder of Forbes magazine once said:

"If you expect nothing, you're apt to be surprised. You'll get it."

If anybody in the world should have reasons for optimism about the future, it's the born-again, blood-washed, Spirit-filled, sanctuary-running, Word-quoting, Bible-thumping children of God.

Yes, you may be going through "stuff" at the moment, but at least you're going "through it" and will soon be on the other side of your mountain of adversity.

God is not surprised by what's going on in your life.

Write that down PLEASE.

God is not surprised by what's going on in my life. Personalize it with your name:

God is not surprised by what's going on in [Name]'s life.

But here's the question:

When trouble comes to visit your home ... what is your response ... <u>do you pull closer to Him</u> ... or revert to the escapism of television or other addictive habits such as a prolonged rendezvous with Ben and Jerry's ice cream.

As I was meditating on this teaching ... God lead me to four scriptures to share with you.

2 Samuel 22:17 in the Message Bible says:

> *"But me he caught—reached all the way from sky to sea; he pulled me out of that ocean of hate, that enemy chaos, the void in which I was drowning. <u>They hit me when I was down, but God stuck by me</u>. He stood me up on a wide-open field; I stood there saved—surprised to be loved!"*

If you've felt like you've been hit when you were already down ... behind on mortgage payments due to slowdowns ... layoffs ... sickness ... then be encouraged by the Word. The God of heaven and earth will stick with you. Can somebody say "Hallelujah."

Be encouraged by Job 5:8-16 in the Message Bible. If you don't have a Message Bible, you can look up the scripture at biblegateway.com. Write it down … put it in your smart phone, tablet or on your legal pad. It's that powerful. Now, here's what the passage says:

> *"[What a Blessing When God Corrects You!] If I were in your shoes, <u>I'd go straight to God</u>, I'd throw myself on the mercy of God. After all, **he's famous for great and unexpected acts; there's no end to his surprises.** He gives rain, for instance, across the wide earth, sends water to irrigate the fields. <u>He raises up the down-and-out, gives firm footing to those sinking in grief.</u> He aborts the schemes of conniving crooks, so that none of their plots come to term. He catches the know-it-alls in their conspiracies—all that intricate intrigue swept out with the trash! Suddenly they're disoriented, plunged into darkness; they can't see to put one foot in front of the other. But <u>the downtrodden are saved by God</u>, saved from the murderous plots, saved from the iron fist. And so <u>the poor continue to hope, while injustice is bound and gagged</u>."*

This scripture in Job tells us seven things we should do if we're hit by a surprise enemy attack.

1. **Go straight to God.**
2. **Ask for His mercy.**
3. **Expect Him to supply every need.**

4. **Remember that God lifts up those who are down.**

5. **Remember that He does not tolerate financial foolishness and cheats.**

6. **Know that God will save you when all seems lost.**

7. **Expect that He will surprise you with His goodness.**

Fast forward four chapters to Job 9:10 in the Message Bible, and you'll read something that should encourage and fill you with anticipation and expectation.

"We'll never comprehend all the great things he does; his miracle-surprises can't be counted."

Hallelujah, but Child of God, YOU, that's right, **YOU must be proactive in bringing these miracle surprises into your life.**

My prayer for you is that you will recall and remember EVERY PROMISE God has made to you in His Word … just as I'm praying for them to be fulfilled in your life.

2 Thessalonians 2:15-17 in the Message Bible says:

"So, friends, take a firm stand, feet on the ground and head high. Keep a tight grip on what you were taught, whether in personal conversation or by our letter. May Jesus himself and God

our Father, who reached out in love and surprised you with gifts of unending help and confidence, put a fresh heart in you, invigorate your work, enliven your speech."

What can God do for you? Here are seven things that God will surprise you with:

1. **Reach out to you in unconditional love.**

2. **Help you now and forever.**

3. **Give you confidence to tackle any challenge or opportunity.**

4. **Wipe all your sins away and give you a fresh heart.**

5. **Empower you for your job … wherever and whatever that may be.**

6. **Anoint your lips to speak the words that He gives you.**

7. **Enable you to stand your ground, with your head held high … confident in His ability to do what He says He will do.**

<u>God is not surprised by what's going on in your world or anywhere else … that's a fact</u>.

Here's something else that's an absolute scriptural fact …

God's just waiting for us not to be surprised by what He will do for us when we get out of the boat

and start walking on the waves of doubt and fear.

God will pull us up out of everything that would pull us down, and that should be no surprise to us.

Just one last thought ... there is no such thing as a surprise miracle.

When you believe for it ... sow for it ... plan for it ... confess it ... anticipate it ... then the manifestation of the thing you most desired from your Heavenly Father will come. And that ... my friends ... should not be a surprise.

Is this your day to sow for a miracle? Do you need miracle manifestation? Go to Sow a Seed at www.haroldherring.com, and sow what God puts on your heart.

Day 26

12 Things God Knows About You

"I know I'm somebody, 'cause God don't make no junk."

Can you say that with me?

"I know I'm somebody, 'cause God don't make no junk."

That powerful quote is by the late, and yes, great Ethel Waters ... an actress and renowned singer who regularly blessed folks with her songs in Billy Graham crusades before her passing in 1977.

Who can ever forget her singing, **"His eye is on the sparrow, and I know He watches me"?**

I want you to personalize this quote from Ms. Waters:

"Harold Herring is somebody, 'cause God don't make no junk."

Now put your name in ... LeJune ... Ray ... Terri ...

I want you to know that what you've just spoken is

much more than just a RICH THOUGHT and confession. It's truth from the Word of God.

I can tell you that **it should be absolutely impossible for any believer or anyone else for that matter to have a poor self-image** if they've read, understood and believed what the Word of God has to say about them.

Ethel Waters was born after her mother was raped at the age of 12. She grew up in poverty, but when she found God, she realized that regardless of her situation, God never makes junk!

There are four powerful verses that prove beyond a shadow of a doubt that you are somebody.

Genesis 1:26 says:

> *"And God said, Let us make man in our image, after our likeness: and let them have dominion over the fish of the sea, and over the fowl of the air, and over the cattle, and over all the earth, and over every creeping thing that creepeth upon the earth."*

Jeremiah 1:5 in the Amplified Bible says:

> *"Before I formed you in the womb I knew [and] approved of you [as My chosen instrument], and before you were born I separated and set you apart, consecrating you; [and] I appointed you*

as a prophet to the nations."

Psalm 139:14 says:

"I will praise thee; for I am fearfully and wonderfully made: marvellous are thy works; and that my soul knoweth right well."

Ephesians 2:10 in the Amplified Bible says:

"For we are God's [own] handiwork (His workmanship), recreated in Christ Jesus, [born anew] that we may do those good works which God predestined (planned beforehand) for us [taking paths which He prepared ahead of time], that we should walk in them [living the good life which He prearranged and made ready for us to live]."

Let's summarize twelve power points from these four verses that reveal what God knows about you.

1. You are made in the image of God and after His likeness.
2. God has given you dominion over everything.
3. God knew you before you were formed in His mother's womb.
4. You are a chosen instrument of God.
5. You are to continually praise God.
6. You are fearfully and wonderfully made.
7. You can do marvelous things through Him.

8. You were personally created by God.
9. You are born again through Christ.
10. God planned in advance for you to do good works.
11. You were created to enjoy the good life that God has prepared.
12. If God is saying all of this to you ... then you've got to know He don't make no junk.

Write out these sentences ... personalize them as a constant reminder of your worth to God.

[Your name] was fearfully and wonderfully created in the image and likeness of God who knew [him, her] before [he, she] was ever formed in [your mother's name]'s womb. God personally created [your name] to continually Praise Him as God gave [your name], a born-again believer, dominion over everything on planet earth and so [he, she] can do the marvelous things God planned in advance and [your name] can enjoy the good life.

Here's my version of those two sentences.

Harold was fearfully and wonderfully created in the image and likeness of God who knew him before he was ever formed in Ms. Annie Ruth's womb. God personally created Harold to continually Praise Him as God gave Harold, a born-again believer, dominion over everything on planet earth and so he can do the marvelous things God planned in advance and Harold can enjoy the good life.

Are you beginning to get the point ... that you're not junk ... that you are in fact somebody ... God's body.

I want you to **personalize four scriptures on an index card or put them in your smart phone.**

Once you've personalized these four verses ... Genesis 1:26; Jeremiah 5:1; Psalm 139:14 and Ephesians 2:10 ... repeat them several times a day.

What you confess ... you will possess.

Now let's go a little further.

As I read Ephesians 2:10, I was also taken by the last part of that verse which says:

> *"... [living the good life which He prearranged and made ready for us to live]."*

God wants you ... that's right ... you to live the good life.

Is living from paycheck to Prozac the good life ... don't think so.

Is never knowing where your spouse or children are the good life ... not a chance.

Is spending your hard-earned money on medications

and doctor's visits the good life ... not the way I read the Word.

Is living in a mortgaged house, sleeping on a bed, watching TV, eating at a table all bought on a payment plan while driving a financed car ... is all of this the good life? Not according to the Word of God.

> The good life according to the Word of God is ...
>
> **Having enough to give what He tells you to give when He tells you to give it and where He tells you to give it.**

2 Corinthians 9:8 in the New King James Version says:

> *"And God is able to make all grace abound toward you, that you, <u>always having all sufficiency in all things</u>, may have an abundance for every good work."*

Walking in divine health is where ... when you take aspirins, the pills feel better.

Exodus 15:26 says:

> *"And said, If thou wilt diligently hearken to the voice of the LORD thy God, and wilt do that which is right in his sight, and wilt give ear to his*

commandments, and keep all his statutes, I will put none of these diseases upon thee, which I have brought upon the Egyptians: for I am the LORD that healeth thee."

The good life is when all your family is serving the Lord.

Acts 16:31 says:

"And they said, Believe on the Lord Jesus Christ, and thou shalt be saved, and thy house."

The good life … is where you have time and the money for family vacations and getaways.

Psalm 68:19 says:

"Blessed be the Lord, who daily loadeth us with benefits, even the God of our salvation. Selah."

The good life is … when you are able to travel on any mission trip with your church regardless of when it occurs.

Acts 13:2 says:

"As they ministered to the Lord, and fasted, the Holy Ghost said, Separate me Barnabas and Saul for the work whereunto I have called them."

Where you can give money to whoever needs some without worrying about your checking account balance … that's the good life.

2 Corinthians 9:11 in the New International Version says:

> "You will be made rich in every way so that you can be generous on every occasion, and through us your generosity will result in thanksgiving to God."

When you find a Godly spouse who understands that husbands and wives are one flesh ... now that's the good life.

Proverbs 19:14 in the Amplified Bible says:

> *"House and riches are the inheritance from fathers, but a wise, understanding, and prudent wife is from the Lord."*

The first key to gaining the good life is realizing who you are in Him ... how He sees you and what He has planned for you ... you will begin to experience the revelation of the 12 things God knows about you.

Day
27

7 Things God Will Do that the Government Can't

I'm tired of negative naysayers ... Christians telling other Christians how bad things are or are going to get economically in this country.

Most of these naysayers are honest and sincere ... however, some are encouraging people to get involved in this investment or that. Some of the naysayers are even seeking to profit from the confusion in the marketplace and on Main Street where people live.

Am I minimizing the economic plight of this country? Absolutely not.

Our government is not just borrowing from Peter to pay Paul. Instead, it's borrowing from Ying to pay Yang (China).

Sadly, **we're borrowing money from people who not only don't serve our God ... they don't believe in God and even fight against Christianity.** These people have nothing but contempt for the American dream and the principles upon which this Republic was founded.

Is that ignorant economic policy? Absolutely.

Is unemployment over 10% when you take out the number of jobs created in the government? Absolutely.

Is unemployment over 15% when you add in the number of people who have stopped looking for jobs or are underemployed? Absolutely.

Is enough being done ... policy-wise ... to spur economic growth and turn things around? Absolutely not.

Is the government continuing to spend more than it takes in? Absolutely.

Is that sound economic policy? Absolutely not. Neither your family nor the government can spend more than they bring in.

> **The bottom line for every family and government is simply this ... if you're in a hole ... stop digging.**

Some people suggest that the only way to turn things around in this country is by redistribution of the people's wealth. Is that an unscriptural idea? Absolutely.

One more thing ... this isn't an issue of Democrats and Republicans ... it's about right and wrong.

Now you're probably wondering if I haven't just confirmed the predictions of the naysayers. Absolutely not.

1 Kings 17:2-4 in the Amplified Bible says:

> *"And the word of the Lord came to him, saying, Go from here and turn east and hide yourself by the brook Cherith, east of the Jordan. You shall drink of the brook, and I have commanded the ravens to feed you there."*

During this period in the history of Israel ... wickedness ruled the land. As punishment ... God brought a famine that lasted for three years.

Times were tough ... economically speaking. Some people were doing without ... but not the prophet Elijah.

God provided for Elijah. He told him exactly where to go and what to do to find the miraculous provision that God provided for him.

During this time period ... God kept the brook from drying up in the midst of a famine. That was huge. God caused the ravens to bring Elijah food ... that was also huge.

Now I want you to visualize and get this next statement down in your spirit.

At a time when people were going hungry in the city ... Elijah was well-fed in the desert.

We need to fully comprehend the fact ... that **as a born-again believer God will provide for us in the midst of an economic famine (hard times) or any other adversity we might face.**

First, we need to know and fully comprehend that God knows our needs.

Matthew 6:32 in the New Living Translation says:

> *"These things dominate the thoughts of unbelievers, but your heavenly Father already knows all your needs."*

Second, God not only knows your needs ... He will supply them.

Philippians 4:19 in the New Living Translation says:

> *"And this same God who takes care of me will supply all your needs from his glorious riches, which have been given to us in Christ Jesus."*

Third, God will tell you where to go and what to do to have your needs met.

Isaiah 48:17 in the New International Version says:

"I am God, your God, who teaches you how to live right and well. I show you what to do, where to go."

Fourth, you must be willing to do what God says regardless of how foolish it might sound.

Although the Word of God doesn't record it ... I'm sure Elijah may have thought ... "What is God thinking sending me to a place in the desert?"

The last place you will expect to find water in a famine is in the desert ... but Elijah was not moved by natural logic ... only by what the Lord said. He, no doubt, knew in his heart that if God said it, he could count on it happening.

Similarly, no one in their natural mind would expect ravens to bring them food. Ravens are scavengers ... they eat whatever they can get their beaks on. But once again, Elijah didn't fret, worry or say anything spiritually ignorant according to the natural mind.

God is not troubled or moved by how desperate our circumstances appear, because He's the solution to every problem we face.

Fifth, we know that God will never leave us without a visible means of support.

Look at the outstanding promises made in Hebrews 13:5 in the Amplified Bible:

> *"Let your character or moral disposition be free from love of money [including greed, avarice, lust, and craving for earthly possessions] and be satisfied with your present [circumstances and with what you have]; for He [God] Himself has said, I will not in any way fail you nor give you up nor leave you without support. [I will] not, [I will] not, [I will] not in any degree leave you helpless nor forsake nor let [you] down (relax My hold on you)! [Assuredly not!]"*

In this verse, we're being told not to put our trust in anything or anybody other than God. Three times God says He will *"not in any way fail you nor give you up nor leave you without support. [I will] not, [I will] not, [I will] not in any degree leave you helpless nor forsake nor let [you] down (relax My hold on you)!"*

Sixth, God will not only support you, but He will give you the desires of your heart.

Psalm 37:4 in the Amplified Bible says:

> *"Delight yourself also in the Lord, and He will give you the desires and secret petitions of your heart."*

When I think of this scripture, I'm also reminded of Matthew 6:21 in the New Living Translation which says:

"Wherever your treasure is, there the desires of your heart will also be."

Seventh, redistribution of wealth is to be done by God and not the government.

The only scriptural redistribution of wealth that is scripturally guaranteed is seedtime and harvest.

Genesis 1:28 says:

"And God blessed them, and God said unto them, Be fruitful, and multiply, and replenish the earth, and subdue it: and have dominion over the fish of the sea, and over the fowl of the air, and over every living thing that moveth upon the earth."

Genesis 26:12 says:

"Then Isaac sowed in that land, and received in the same year an hundredfold: and the LORD blessed him."

Galatians 6:7 in the Amplified Bible says:

"Do not be deceived and deluded and misled; God will not allow Himself to be sneered at (scorned, disdained, or mocked by mere pretensions or professions, or by His precepts being set aside). [He inevitably deludes himself who attempts to delude God.] For whatever a man

sows, that and that only is what he will reap."

The scripture says what "we sow" that "we shall reap." It's not what somebody else sows ... it's what *we* sow.

In summary, here's my economic policy:

First, God, not the government, will solve your problems ... if you trust Him and obey His instructions.

Second, no matter how bleak things may look ... God will ALWAYS, ALWAYS provide for your needs and desires (Hebrews 13:5).

Third, put your confidence in the only One who can bring financial deliverance to your house.

Day 28

7 Things About God's Will For You

Let's talk about one of the most misunderstood scriptures in the Word of God.

Romans 8:28 says:

> *"And we know that all things work together for good to them that love God, to them who are the called according to his purpose."*

During the first part of my walk with the Lord ... that verse was used most often as a healing balm for the tragedies of life.

If someone was killed in an automobile accident, then *"... all things work together for good to them that love God, to them who are the called according to his purpose."*

How do you explain to a parent who has had a child abducted or kidnapped ... that it's working to their good?

How do you explain to a husband whose wife was killed by a drunk driver … that it's working to his good?

How do you explain to a congregation that lost its pastor to sexual sin … that it's working to their good?

Rather than go through a long discourse of bad things happening to good people being justifiable or acceptable by throwing Romans 8:28 at the problem … let me simply say, that's not what that verse means.

Yes, we do need to find comfort in the midst of loss and tragedy … but it needs to be spiritually sound and not just something that sounds pious but does nothing to soothe the hurting person's grief.

Let's look at Romans 8:28 again, but this time let's also look at it in context with Verses 27 and 29. This is what the Amplified Bible says:

"And He Who searches the hearts of men knows what is in the mind of the [Holy] Spirit [what His intent is], because the Spirit intercedes and pleads [before God] in behalf of the saints according to and in harmony with God's will.

"We are assured and know that [God being a partner in their labor] all things work together and are [fitting into a plan] for good to and for those who love God and are called according to [His] design and purpose.

"For those whom He foreknew [of whom He was aware and loved beforehand], He also destined from the beginning [foreordaining them] to be molded into the image of His Son [and share inwardly His likeness], that He might become the firstborn among many brethren."

Verse 27 says: "… *knows what is in the mind of the [Holy] Spirit [what His intent is] …"*

<u>Do you think the intent of the Holy Spirit is to inflict pain and suffering on anyone by tragic events</u>? Is that working toward your good? Of course not.

The Holy Spirit "… *pleads [before God] in behalf of the saints according to and in harmony with God's will …"*

It is never God's will for you live in anguish, hoping it will work good in your life.

What is God's will for your life? Here are seven things to consider.

1. You should be born again.

John 3:16 says:

"For God so loved the world, that he gave his only begotten Son, that whosoever believeth in him should not perish, but have everlasting life."

2 Peter 3:9 in the Amplified Bible says:

"The Lord does not delay and is not tardy or slow about what He promises, according to some people's conception of slowness, but He is long-suffering (extraordinarily patient) toward you, not desiring that any should perish, but that all should turn to repentance."

2. You should live a holy and righteous life.

Hebrews 10:10 in the New Living Translation says:

"For God's will was for us to be made holy by the sacrifice of the body of Jesus Christ, once for all time."

3. You should walk in divine health.

Matthew 8:16-17 in the Amplified Bible says:

"When evening came, they brought to Him many who were under the power of demons, and He drove out the spirits with a word and restored to health all who were sick.

"And thus He fulfilled what was spoken by the prophet Isaiah, He Himself took [in order to carry away] our weaknesses and infirmities and bore away our diseases."

4. You should operate in the gifts of the Spirit.

1 Corinthians 12:7-11 in the Amplified Bible says:

"But to each one is given the manifestation of the [Holy] Spirit [the evidence, the spiritual illumination of the Spirit] for good and profit.

"To one is given in and through the [Holy] Spirit [the power to speak] a message of wisdom, and to another [the power to express] a word of knowledge and understanding according to the same [Holy] Spirit;

"To another [wonder-working] faith by the same [Holy] Spirit, to another the extraordinary powers of healing by the one Spirit;

"To another the working of miracles, to another prophetic insight (the gift of interpreting the divine will and purpose); to another the ability to discern and distinguish between [the utterances of true] spirits [and false ones], to another various kinds of [unknown] tongues, to another the ability to interpret [such] tongues.

"All these [gifts, achievements, abilities] are inspired and brought to pass by one and the same [Holy] Spirit, Who apportions to each person individually [exactly] as He chooses."

5. You will live a life controlled by the fruit of the Spirit.

Galatians 5:22-25 in the Amplified Bible says:

> "But the fruit of the [Holy] Spirit [the work which His presence within accomplishes] is love, joy (gladness), peace, patience (an even temper, forbearance), kindness, goodness (benevolence), faithfulness,
>
> "Gentleness (meekness, humility), self-control (self-restraint, continence). Against such things there is no law [that can bring a charge].
>
> "And those who belong to Christ Jesus (the Messiah) have crucified the flesh (the godless human nature) with its passions and appetites and desires.
>
> "If we live by the [Holy] Spirit, let us also walk by the Spirit. [If by the Holy Spirit we have our life in God, let us go forward walking in line, our conduct controlled by the Spirit.]"

6. You will live a life that is pleasing to the Lord.

Ephesians 5:8-10 in the Amplified Bible says:

> "For once you were darkness, but now you are light in the Lord; walk as children of Light [lead the lives of those native-born to the Light].
>
> "For the fruit (the effect, the product) of the Light

or the Spirit [consists] in every form of kindly goodness, uprightness of heart, and trueness of life.

"And try to learn [in your experience] what is pleasing to the Lord [let your lives be constant proofs of what is most acceptable to Him]."

7. You walk in the realm of the miraculous.

Galatians 3:5 in the Amplified Bible says:

"Then does He Who supplies you with His marvelous [Holy] Spirit and works powerfully and miraculously among you do so on [the grounds of your doing] what the Law demands, or because of your believing in and adhering to and trusting in and relying on the message that you heard?"

> ## This list could go on and on.

We can know that all things are working together for good when we are manifesting everything that He created and preordained for us.

When we live our lives in such a way that we're fulfilling our destiny and glorifying Him, then truly we are called according to His purpose.

The key to all things working together for good is found in Romans 12:2. The New Living Translation says it this way:

> *"Don't copy the behavior and customs of this world, but let God transform you into a new person by changing the way you think. Then you will learn to know God's will for you, which is good and pleasing and perfect."*

Hallelujah and amen!!

Write It Down

Day 29

Do you keep a journal of God's blessings in your life?

Do you regularly write about the things God is showing you in His Word?

Do you keep written records of your journey to the debt free lifestyle?

If not, you might want to start. The Word of God says in Numbers 33:1-2 in the New Living Translation:

> *"This is the route the Israelites followed as they marched out of Egypt under the leadership of Moses and Aaron. At the Lord's direction, Moses kept a written record of their progress. These are the stages of their march, identified by the different places where they stopped along the way."*

In reading this passage of scripture there are some who will immediately think that doesn't apply to me because I've never been to Egypt. But the truth of the matter is <u>way too many believers are living in a</u>

<u>spiritual Egypt where their life is not their own</u>.

Spiritual Egypt produces a lifestyle where you never have enough. It's a place where you live from pay-check to paycheck. If you don't work ... you don't eat. A place where you will always be working for "the other guy."

Spiritual Egypt is also a place where you are sub-jected to every whim of the cruel taskmasters.

When I said cruel taskmaster ... many of you caught a visual of the cruel Egyptian taskmaster that Moses killed in the movie *The Ten Commandments.*

In the 21st century, cruel taskmasters don't come with straw, rationed food, a whip and the bondage of slave labor.

> Today's taskmasters are our creditors who charge high interest rates, change the rules of the credit card and give out bad credit scores all the while making us their personal slave, causing us <u>to live lives controlled by someone else</u>.

The nature of our relationship to our creditors is very clearly defined in Proverbs 22:7 in the Contemporary English Version of the Bible which says:

"The poor are ruled by the rich, and those who

borrow are slaves of moneylenders."

So, it's very clear … if you're in debt, you're a slave to the taskmasters, the money lenders, the creditors.

But the very good news is … you can leave spiritual Egypt. God wants you to journey, and yes, *journal* from your current location to the Promised Land that He has for you.

And just for the record, I'm not taking about Heaven as your Promised Land, although it is, of course, our ultimate destination.

John 10:10 says:

> *"The thief cometh not, but for to steal, and to kill, and to destroy: I am come that they might have life, and that they might have it more abundantly."*

Jesus came that you and I might have life … that means today … right now. He came that we might have life and have it more abundantly.

In fact, John 10:10 in the New Living Translation says it this way:

> *"… My purpose is to give them a rich and satisfying life."*

So there is no question about which direction God wants you to take … it's toward a "rich and satisfying life" now. He wants us on a journey to a life free of credit taskmasters so we can experience the debt free life.

But He gave us some very specific instructions as to what we should be doing on this journey. Let's look at Numbers 33:2 in the New Living Translation once again.

> "At the Lord's direction, Moses kept a written record of their progress. These are the stages of their march, identified by the different places where they stopped along the way."

God wants you to keep a written record of the progress you're making on your journey. Why would He make such a request? Here are four reasons why God wants you to keep a journal.

1. To remind you of where you came from.

Sadly, many people forget what they've been delivered of or out of ... and how God has blessed and kept them.

> Remembering where we came from should stir compassion in us for the plight of others and what they're going through. <u>The journal of the past should be written with thoughts of praise and thanksgiving for what God has done in our lives</u>.

In biblical Egypt, a taskmaster could destroy a home by taking a daughter for his wife and/or mistress. In spiritual Egypt, a credit taskmaster can destroy a family by taking away financial peace and replacing it with financial stress.

2. To remind you of where you're going.

Exodus 3:8 in the New Living Translation says:

"So I have come down to rescue them from the power of the Egyptians and lead them out of Egypt into their own fertile and spacious land. It is a land flowing with milk and honey ..."

God had promised the children of Israel the Promised Land as an inheritance.

Leviticus 20:24 in the New Living Translation says:

"But I have promised you, 'You will possess their land because I will give it to you as your possession—a land flowing with milk and honey.' I am the Lord your God, who has set you apart from all other people."

As a child of the Most High God ... the seed of Abraham ... your Heavenly Father has also made promises to you ... on your journey to the debt free lifestyle. Here are four scriptures that speak of your financial future in your Promised Land.

Insert your name into these verses.

Deuteronomy 8:18 says:

> *"But thou shalt remember the LORD thy God: for it is he that giveth [YourName] power to get wealth, that he may establish his covenant which he sware unto thy fathers, as it is this day."*

3 John 1:2 says:

> *"I pray that [YourName] may prosper in all things and be in good health, even as [Your Name]'s soul prospers."*

Proverbs 10:22 says:

> *"The Lord's blessings brings wealth to [Your Name], And He adds no trouble to it."*

Psalm 112:3 says:

> *"Wealth and riches shall be in [Your Name]'s house: and [his, her, their] righteousness endureth for ever."*

3. To remind you of what you went through to get there.

The children of Israel went through a lot in the wilderness ... unfortunately, it was a result of their own actions.

Today, many of God's children are in a spiritual

wilderness of their own creation. Regardless of how you got in the mess you're in … God will show you the way out if you follow His direction.

Psalm 66:12 says:

> *"Thou hast caused men to ride over our heads; we went through fire and through water: but thou broughtest us out into a wealthy place."*

4. To remind you of how He never left your side during the journey.

I felt led to share 2 Corinthians 4:7-12 in the Message Bible which says:

> *"… We've been surrounded and battered by troubles, but we're not demoralized; we're not sure what to do, but we know that God knows what to do; we've been spiritually terrorized, but God hasn't left our side; we've been thrown down, but we haven't broken. What they did to Jesus, they do to us—trial and torture, mockery and murder; what Jesus did among them, he does in us—he lives …"*

Wow … that's something to think about, be thankful for and write about as you put some distance between you and your spiritual Egypt.

As a reminder … if you haven't read … the seven things to do before you go to sleep, do so immediately

… if you've read it already … ask yourself a question.

Are you doing what it says?

Dr. Anita from Virginia emailed me to say …

"Sunday night and Monday I wrote down my daily confessions.

"I received discounts on tires for my truck, and a gift when purchasing a new wallet after the old one broke while flying back home.

"I did the declaration of the next morning and scheduled my activity. I experienced a day with favors, kindness from people, surprises, and provisions.

"It was a glorious day."

If God will do this for Dr. Anita … you can rest assured … he will do it for you.

Day 30

Get Out Of Your Rut Now

God brought Isaiah 43:19 to my remembrance. It says:

> *"Behold, I will do a new thing; now it shall spring forth; shall ye not know it? I will even make a way in the wilderness, and rivers in the desert."*

The Lord wants to do a "new thing" in your life. Unfortunately, He can't get through to some folks because they enjoy living in the past. They must enjoy it, because they spend so much time there.

If you dwell on past hurts, failures, broken relation-ships and financial mistakes, then truly you're doomed to repeat them.

I think <u>one of the primary reasons people fail is because they're dwelling on past memories and experiences</u>.

The Message Bible translation of Isaiah 43:18 says:

> *"Forget about what's happened; don't keep go-ing over old history. Be alert, be present."*

There's a reason God put our eyes in the front of our head instead of the back. He wants us looking forward.

There is only one time in the Bible that somebody looked back longingly to a past life while trying to walk forward. It didn't work for her, and it won't work for you either.

Genesis 19:26 in the New Living Translation says:

"But Lot's wife looked back as she was following behind him, and she turned into a pillar of salt."

Unfortunately, <u>sometimes living in the past becomes so familiar that it becomes a comfort zone ... a routine</u>.

There's a tendency for us to do the same thing over and over again because it's what we've always done.

We get up at the same time each morning ... get ready the same way ... eat the same thing for breakfast ... drive to work along the same route ... listen to the same radio station ... arrive at work at the same time ... do the same thing on our job ... take a break at the same time ... sit with the same people ... go to lunch at the same time ... talk about the same things with co-workers ... get off work at the same time ... arrive home at the same time ... do the same things before and after dinner ... watch the same television programs ... go to bed at the same time ... so we can do all the same things again tomorrow.

Don't get me wrong … there are certain things you have to do and want to do the same way, but where do you create time for God to do a new thing … to get out of the routine?

It's been said that a routine is a rut … and **a rut is just a grave with the ends knocked out.**

God cannot do a new thing in our lives as long as we're living in the past or in a rut.

There are three questions everyone should ask themselves if they want to overcome the ruts of life and allow God to do a new thing.

First, is this a rut of our own creation?

Sometimes we tend to live in a rut, because there is no risk of failure. It is, however, a fact that without a risk of failure there can never be a reward. Doing a new thing sometimes requires a risk.

Second, understand who we're following.

Many people fall into a work rut, because they got a job where their parents or best friends work. If we're going to follow the crowd … make sure we know where the crowd is going … and that it all lines up with the Word of God and His purpose for our life.

Third, we need to ask ourselves where we're going.

Are we ready if God decides to do a new thing in us? Or are we happy to go along to get along?

Have we discovered our purpose?

Do we have a vision for its manifestation and goals for its implementation?

It's time to forget the past ... break free of our ruts ... so God can do a new thing.

Philippians 3:13 says:

> *"Brethren, I count not myself to have apprehended: but **this one thing I do**, forgetting those things which are behind, and reaching forth unto those things which are before."*

The Apostle Paul was a man with vast knowledge of the Word, one who saw signs and wonders following his travels ... one who raised up disciples ... one who endured extreme persecution ... and he speaks of one thing that he did.

> *"... forgetting those things which are behind, and reaching forth unto those things which are before."*

Paul was reaching out to new things ... new opportunities ... new places ... new people. He was not living in the past ... if there was ever anyone who could have lived in the past, it was the Apostle Paul. But the scripture says that he left the past in the past, and he journeyed on toward a new thing.

Philippians 3:14 says:

> *"I press toward the mark for the prize of the high calling of God in Christ Jesus."*

If you want the prize ... to hear God say ... "Well-done my good and faithful servant" ... then you've got to forget the past ... reach out to do new things ... without looking back.

In Verse 14, the Message Bible says: *"... I'm off and running, and I'm not turning back."*

As you begin to do a new thing in your life ... make sure you're not bringing along any extra, bulky, heavy and totally useless baggage. If there are people you need to forgive and forget ... just do it.

Unforgiveness will literally destroy your future ... causing you to live in the bitterness of yesteryear.

It's interesting the Spell Check function on the Microsoft Word program I'm using highlighted unforgiveness as a misspelled world. When I clicked the word to check for a proper spelling, forgiveness popped up. It wasn't in the program's dictionary until I added it.

In other words, we have a choice ... whether or not we allow unforgiveness into our vocabulary and our life. And just for the record, the word unforgiveness is not in the Bible. Forgiveness is, but not unforgiveness.

I believe it's because God doesn't want that word in our vocabulary.

God wants to do a new thing in your life ... something fresh ... full of His glory and power ... but He can't if you're focused on past hurts.

Philippians 3:15-16 in the Message Bible says:

> "So _let's keep focused on that goal,_ **those of us who want everything God has for us.** If any of you have something else in mind, something less than total commitment, God will clear your blurred vision—you'll see it yet! Now that we're on the right track, let's stay on it."

If you're serious about your future ... take a few minutes to write out and reflect on your answers to the three questions I posed about overcoming ruts. Completing the exercise will allow God to "... clear your blurred vision."

With the kind of future God has in store for you ... why would you ever want to look in the rear view mirror of your life, where the picture is limited and passing, when you can look forward to a vast vista of something new and exciting.

If you want to travel down the highway of life with God ... stop looking back ... forget the past ... anticipate Him doing a new thing in your life ... the whole world lies before you.

Get out of your rut ... so you can get into the new thing God wants to do in your life.

It bears repeating once more ... his new thing will be ... **something fresh** ... and **full of his glory and power** ... and that makes me want **to jump and shout!!!**

Day 31

When God Takes No Pleasure in You

God wants our best … He desires we put forth our best effort … not just seeing what we can get by with.

It's the way we show God that we desire to be holy as He is holy.

Consider the words of Leviticus 1:3 in the Amplified Bible:

> *"If his offering is a burnt offering from the herd, he shall offer a male <u>without blemish</u>; he shall offer it at the door of the Tent of Meeting, that he may be accepted before the Lord."*

The word for *blemish* is **tamiym** (H8549) and is also defined as "perfect."

The sacrifices needed to be perfect because they symbolized holiness. The Book of Leviticus is primarily about Hebrew worship (how it was done, who was to lead it and the kind of sacrifices to be offered), all leading to holiness.

The children of Israel were told to take the very best of their male animals and offer them as the blood sacrifice.

The natural mind ... the business mind ... would have preferred to sacrifice the weak, the imperfect, the blemished ones while holding back the best in hopes of improving the gene pool of the flock.

This scripture in Leviticus is very clear ... **if you want your offering to be acceptable, then you'd better bring your best.**

If God was asking for the best ... then the children of Israel had to trust God to replenish their herds with perfection.

God never requires a sacrificial gift without giving something greater in return. That's who He is and how He conducts business.

The same requirements were involved in the offering of grain. The flour had to be the finest milled.

In short, **the quality of a person's sacrifice determined their reverence for God and personal commitment to live a life of holiness before Him.**

After the children of Israel returned from exile ... God got even more specific about how He felt about those who offered blind, lame and diseased animals for sacrifice. God wasn't happy ... in fact, He said that people who gave less than their best "despised His name."

Malachi 1:6 in the Amplified Bible says:

> *"A son honors his father, and a servant his master. If then I am a Father, where is My honor? And if I am a Master, where is the [reverent] fear due Me? says the Lord of hosts to you, O priests, who despise My name. You say, How and in what way have we despised Your name?"*

The New Living Translation of Malachi 1:6 says:

> *"… You have shown contempt for my name! But you ask, 'How have we ever shown contempt for your name?' "*

No matter which translation we use … it's pretty clear God is not happy.

Truthfully, they should have known why He wasn't happy, but He spells it out in Malachi 1:7, which states:

> *"By offering polluted food upon My altar. And you ask, How have we polluted it and profaned You? By thinking that the table of the Lord is contemptible and may be despised."*

God not only wants the best … He wants to be first. Let's look further at Malachi 1:7-8 in the Message Bible:

> *"When you say, 'The altar of God is not important anymore; worship of God is no longer a*

priority,' that's defiling. And when you offer worthless animals for sacrifices in worship, animals that you're trying to get rid of—blind and sick and crippled animals—isn't that defiling? Try a trick like that with your banker or your senator—how far do you think it will get you? ..."

When we fail to give God our best ... not only is He not happy about it but the scripture says He will not even accept the offering.

A church or ministry may accept an offering of less than your best, but God does not.

Malachi 1:10 in the Amplified Bible says:

"Oh, that there were even one among you [whose duty it is to minister to Me] who would shut the doors, that you might not kindle fire on My altar to no purpose [an empty, futile, fruitless pretense]! I have no pleasure in you, says the Lord of hosts, nor will I accept an offering from your hand."

There are a lot of things that I'd like to hear God say about me ... but **I can tell you that I NEVER EVER want to hear Him say that He has no pleasure in me.**

The Message Bible translation of Malachi 1:11 says:

"... And there are people who know how to worship me all over the world, who honor me by

bringing their best to me."

I think the scripture is clear that God was not happy when the Hebrew children offered Him less than their best. From these references, we can conclude that when it comes to our offerings and the lives we live for Him, He is expecting our best, too.

You might be thinking, "I would never do that. I would never insult God by giving him an offering that is sick, lame, defective or less than my best."

Since we don't offer animals for sacrifice, we may not think this is relevant to us, but let's come back to that question in a moment.

Malachi 1:14 in the Message Bible says:

"A curse on the person who makes a big show of doing something great for me—an expensive sacrifice, say—and then at the last minute brings in something puny and worthless! I'm a great king … honored far and wide, and I'll not put up with it!"

I find it interesting that this verse says that a switch was made at the last minute.

Now let's go to Matthew 21:12 which says:

"And Jesus went into the temple of God, and cast out all them that sold and bought in the temple, and overthrew the tables of the money-

changers, and the seats of them that sold doves."

The merchants in the courtyard were selling animals for sacrifice. This was done as a convenience for those who left home without their sacrifice or perhaps decided to change the kind of animal they were sacrificing at the last minute.

Jesus was not ignorant of the fact that this practice was set up in the Temple because people were too lazy to bring their best from home, or as an excuse to offer an animal that was less than the best.

Evidently some of the moneychangers were even using less than honest scales, for in Verse 13 of Matthew 21, Jesus calls it "a den of thieves."

Proverbs 20:23 in the Message Bible translation says:

"God hates cheating in the marketplace; rigged scales are an outrage."

Honesty in the marketplace is also mentioned in Proverbs 11:1 in the Message Bible which says:

"God hates cheating in the marketplace; he loves it when business is aboveboard."

There were three things that upset Jesus about what was going on in the courtyard.

First, the moneychangers were cheating people.

Second, the moneychangers were selling animals for sacrifice that were less than the best.

And third, I might as well say it again ... **God takes no pleasure in offerings that are not properly given no matter what the reason.**

When the pastor takes a special offering, or when you're reading a partner letter from the Debt Free Army or some other ministry ... are you giving less than your best?

Do you pray and ask God what He would have you give? I can assure you that God will never have you sow less than your best.

The question is not what He wants ... but what you do in response to what He wants.

God wants your best ... in every area ... at home, on the job and in your family relationships.

When you come before Him, it is to your benefit to come with your best.

RichThoughts for Breakfast
Volume 5

Invite Harold Herring to speak at your church, event, or rally.

Keep Thinking Rich Thoughts,

Harold Herring